The author's titles also published by Vagabond Voices are:

In Place of Fear II (2014)

In Place of Failure (2015)

The New Case for Optimism

Jim Sillars

Vagabond Voices
Glasgow

First published in November 2025 by
Vagabond Voices Publishing Ltd.,
Glasgow,
Scotland.

ISBN 978-1-913212-42-1

Printed and bound in Poland
Cover design by Mark Mechan
Typeset by Raspberry Creative Type

For further information on Vagabond Voices, see the website,
www.vagabondvoices.co.uk

This book is dedicated to Iain Lawson, a friend with whom I was privileged to campaign, and whose death I continue to mourn

Acknowledgements

I am indebted to Alex Neil, Professor Joe Farrell, Peter Kearney, and Calum Miller for the time they have spent discussing the matters addressed in this book, for their encouragement to continue writing when I was flagging, and their critical assessment and comments on its earlier drafts. What this book contains, however, are my views and my views alone.

I also wish to express my thanks to Professor Lindsay Paterson for meeting me to discuss the Scottish education system, and for the papers he directed my attention to.

I am indebted to two people for the assistance given to me in areas where research was required, and where my own efforts needed to be double-checked. One is Jim Eadie, a lifelong friend, the other is Ariane Loening whose diligent research on climate issues I have borrowed, not only for this book, but for other written material under my name.

My thanks are due also to Allan Cameron, my editor and publisher, without whose commitment and help this book would never have seen the light of day.

Alex Neil, Joe Farrell, Lindsay Paterson were, along with me, founder members of the SLP. I don't think any of us regret trying to establish a genuine independent Scottish Labour Party, despite us failing. It is still needed.

Author's Note

The SNP decision to help bring down the Callaghan Labour government in the no confidence vote of 1979, and so usher in the deindustrialisation that was a consequence of Margaret Thatcher's government, produced not just a heavy defeat in the election that followed, but years of bitterness towards it from Scotland's people. Morale among SNP activists, and those who supported independence outside of its ranks, was low in the following years. Things were not much better in the Labour party in Scotland. They had a majority of MPs, won on an anti-Thatcher ticket, but could do nothing. Alex Salmond coined a telling label to describe them: The Feeble Fifty.

I took a different view from most, based on analysis of what had happened between 1974 and 1979, when the SNP appeared to be an unstoppable force but ended up in an almighty crash. Taking account of the inexperience of the party at that time in the big league of Westminster politics, and the errors that flowed from that inexperience, together with a view of what could be done to restore confidence in the movement, led me to write *The Case for Optimism* in 1986. I have learned subsequently that it had a positive impact on the independence movement. Two years later came the seminal SNP victory in the Govan by-election.

Today the SNP and the movement are in a different position to that in the 1980s. The 2014 referendum was a legal defeat but a political victory, in that the campaign built an independence base of hardcore support of 45 per cent; one that delivered spectacular electoral success to the SNP in 2015. Despite setbacks since then, the SNP is still the government of devolved Scotland. As I write, opinion polls show that despite only showing now at around 30% voting support, it is still the majority party heading into the 2026 Holyrood elections.

There were reasons for that 2014 referendum result failing in its principal aim. The case for independence was not well prepared, with the issue on currency being the most obvious example. Today, there are serious questions about the SNP's ability to lead and succeed in gaining independence.

Outside of the SNP there now exists a broad active movement. Yet we appear to be stuck. There is no outreach to the people. There is frustration. This book is intended to look, explain and explore the issues that can help us not only become unstuck, but emerge with a better case for independence than that presented in 2014. I look to 2028-29 as the decisive period.

Introduction

The new case for optimism on independence is based on a different perception now from what mattered in the debate in 2014 when Scots were urged to stay under the umbrella of the big, economically powerful United Kingdom, upon which we had to depend.

Today, the imperative for Scotland is to escape from a decaying British state, which can offer us nothing but a share in its decline.

This book identifies who really matters if victory is to be achieved – the unionists, whom we need to convert. It invites Scots to assess the important geopolitical influences that need to be recognised, and reflects upon the governance of the parliament at Holyrood, the quality and experience lacking in those who serve in its devolutionist form at present, together with what will be required when it sits as a representative legislature of a sovereign state.

Emphasis will be on the concept of Scottish state interests, and how for the first time in over 300 years these must now dominate Scotland's thinking and actions.

A good part of the book, Chapter 12, will be the demolition of Devo-Max or Home Rule as adumbrated by Ben Thomson in his book ***Scottish Home Rule: The ANSWER to Scotland's Constitutional Question***, which is the best case for that proposition I have read.

The reason for devoting time and space to Devo-Max, or Quasi-Federalism as it might also be named, is that this is the policy I anticipate Westminster will advance when next we have a referendum, and those who will lead the independence movement at that time should be well prepared now to combat it.

Local government, just as important as the legislature, will come into focus in terms of its powers, and how we see and pay our councillors.

The views I express in Chapter 7 on the issue of climate change, which is real, and the wrong-headed demonisation of fossil fuels and CO_2 as the culprit, will upset some who have bought into what can only be described as propaganda masquerading as scientific consensus. The chapter on Scotland's economy points to the importance of North Sea oil and gas as an essential source of the capital that will be required if an independent parliament and government are to transform Scotland's current low wage, low investment, and low productivity economy into one that is dynamic and achieves higher living standards.

Last but by no means least is an understanding of why the Labour party and its voters, both important to win over to our cause, are still reluctant to move from devolution to independence.

What up to now has been the electoral wing of the movement, the SNP, has not covered itself in glory as a government at Holyrood in the past decade. As noted earlier, its standing in the opinion polls in the low-thirties, while enough for it to remain the majority party, is far from the level of mandate required to rally the nation to call for and accomplish independence. Its leadership has drawn praise from unionist writers for having sidelined independence. It is indicative of the state of Scottish politics, and of the SNP, that in the March 2025 assessment of political leaders John Swinney was described as the "most popular" with a negative rating of -14, when compared to Anas Sarwar at -29.

The vacuum created by poor SNP leadership since 2014 has seen the movement split, splintered and in a pathological condition with sections of it going down every rabbit hole available.

So where, in that apparently bleak political landscape on which the Sun seems to have set, is there any case for optimism?

There is such a case. A compelling case. But if independence is to happen, we need to look at why we are in apparent failure, correct the errors that led us here, rebuild the political structures, and produce an honest policy prospectus based on priorities; one above all that is capable of persuading a sufficient number of Unionists that it is in their interest too to embrace independence.

We are not here in the dumps because of some superb unionist manoeuvre, or by accident, but by error on the part of an unaccountable SNP leadership and a membership that wallowed in the cult of personality, swallowing what its intelligence should have told it was false, and thus abdicated its responsibility to tell fact from fiction, PR from policy.

It was not independence that was felled on 4th July 2024; it was not the idea of independence that was tarnished in the wasted decade since 2014, but the party of independence and its leadership and membership, which carried responsibility for delivering it. It is unlikely that the SNP leadership will admit to its contribution to defeat. I saw no signs of that in the private session of the party's 2024 conference. If the membership too cannot accept that its role as the happy-clappy encore to mediocrity was a major factor in disaster, then the movement may come to the conclusion that the SNP should abdicate its lead position.

Right up to 2014, the SNP earned its position as the political party with the right to lead the independence movement, because of its record in keeping itself alive and advancing the cause despite morale-sapping periods of electoral defeat and its success in forming a competent administration from 2007-2014. That right was earned. It is a key question whether that right continues to exist.

Below the media radar, and despite the propensity of some to find those rabbit holes, the independence movement is alive. Various groups are engaged in serious policy work, each aiming to produce solid material upon which a future independence campaign can succeed in gaining a referendum, and winning it by a substantial margin. An example is those working on currency, whose latest examination of this crucial matter attracted an audience of 350, including experts from other countries. Work by another group on the economy is impressive.

The need to get the work they are doing out to the public requires the creation of a national campaign organisation able to promote and disseminate a comprehensive set of policies for a transformational independent Scotland. That will happen. Whether such a national organisation, reflecting the breadth and depth of the whole movement, will be content to accept the SNP as the lead electoral instrument of the movement is an open question.

Jim Sillars
Edinburgh,
July 2025

The New Case for Optimism

Chapter One
Scottish state interests

"Nations have no permanent friends or allies; they only have permanent interests"
Lord Palmerston

Unionists believe independence has been killed off with the 2024 Westminster election result, and the dialling down on the issue by the SNP government since then.

Unionists are wrong. The balance between retaining the link with England and escaping from it with independence has changed. The latter now has a distinct advantage. Many have still to see what is obvious: Scotland is a junior partner within a state in its final stages of imperial decline, a state that is poor pretending to be rich, and a state that is broke and broken. A failing England, the giant part of the state of 58m, that Scotland's 5.4m cannot save. Scotland can only save itself by departing from the union.

There are two important points people in Scotland need to grasp.

First is the true nature of the British state. The UK is and always has been since 1707 the English state with a Scottish appendage. Not a colony, a union construct of English political genius – a supposedly new state created by two states merging as one. The new Parliament elected in 1708 contained 513 MPs from England, 45 from Scotland, with 16 Scottish Peers admitted to the House of Lords containing 191 English ones. It was, in fact, the English Parliament continuing, with previous English Parliament rules in place.

Legally the 1708 Parliament was the first Parliament of Great. Britain. But the reality of the English Parliament continuing, with its rules in force, was the realpolitik fact. That fact was underlined in 1965, when we were enjoined to celebrate the seven hundredth anniversary of the establishment of Parliament and seven hundred and fiftieth anniversary of Magna Carta, both rooted in English history.

What the English got from the union was the admittance of 45 Scots to its Parliament while gaining an important piece of territory and a source of human talent both civil and military, which were employed to advance English state interests in extending its imperial ambitions.

Second, the policy of "managed decline" practised by the English state's elite since 1945 has given way to accelerated decline delivered by two major shocks: the 2007-8 financial crisis when government saved the banks but plunged the people into austerity, and the mishandling of the Covid pandemic resulting in the trashing of the economy.

England has not only become poorer (and Scotland along with it, an inevitability from being part of the union) but it is also a divided and unhappy country with sectarianism now embedded in its political life, and represented in the Westminster Parliament for the first time. Despite genuine efforts to make multiculturalism work, in many parts of England people live in different political and cultural silos.

Little attention has been paid to the long-term implications of the 2024 election results that show the potential impact of this new sectarianism. Perhaps that is because people in England, especially those in leadership positions, don't want to see and admit it. But look at Wes Streeting, by any measure a major politician. In his constituency in 2019 he won 50.5% of the vote, in 2024 he scraped back to Parliament with a majority of 528. Jonathan Ashworth, senior shadow cabinet member, saw his 22,000-majority demolished and was defeated. Both were opposed by sectarian candidates, from among the 300 that contested constituencies. There were a number of other close shaves for Labour MPs. The Labour Government's reaction has been to seek an accepted definition of Islamophobia, seen by many as a backdoor law of blasphemy for one religion alone, and thus divisive.

If I am correct in reading the future of England, and I believe I am, it will be a very unhappy and increasingly disunited country. It is not in Scotland's people's or in Scotland's long term state interests, to remain attached to England as it is now developing.

This is not the beginning of an anti-English diatribe. I write in the context of something the Scots have paid no attention to for over 300 years – Scottish state interests. Nothing in my record shows any animus towards the English nation. Indeed, although an atheist, the Hym Jerusalem, is my favourite piece of music. Aside from me liking the it, the words, an anthem of England, describe a country that was, but is no more.

I have no resentment against English state interests having been the dominant factor in British state activity. It could not have been otherwise given the lopsided nature of the union. Had the proportions of population been different with Scotland the giant and England the minnow, Scots would have acted principally in the Scottish interest. Realpolitik on the island of Great Britain did not disappear in 1707. It continued.

Nor do I wail over 1707 and curse Burns' parcel of rogues. It was imperative policy for England to close the border for foreign policy and defence reasons, and thus deny France the use of its Scottish proxy to make serious trouble. I often wonder as I hear people talk of the Auld Alliance in sentimental terms, if they realise it cost France nothing to bait the English with its Scottish proxy, while the Scots often paid a heavy price.

The English Aliens Act 1705 was step one towards that union objective, and one cannot blame the English for seizing the opportunity of the next step once Scotland's men of business and finance ruined themselves with the Darien scheme. 1707 was a triumph of English foreign policy.

Nor do I deny that Scotland, and a considerable number of Scots, in becoming part of the English dominated British state, benefitted from its imperial ambitions, driven to success in no small part by the explosion of science and technology let loose by the industrial revolution. The Scottish administrative, merchant, banking, manufacturing, and aristocratic classes were the main beneficiaries from the union. The working classes too were transformed from life in agriculture to new skilled jobs in the new economy, but were not beneficiaries in wealth-accumulation or high living standards as were the others. That story of imperial benefits started coming to an end in the long slide downwards following World War II.

In 1707, those in charge of Scotland, after the Darien disaster, saw Scottish state interests as best served by joining with England politically and economically in a union that gave Scots unhindered access to a larger domestic market, and access to a growing imperial one.

That was then. This is now. The union no longer serves a purpose for Scottish state interests, which is the interests of its people now and in the future. Our state interests, properly addressed, compel us to part company from a partner no longer able to offer us access to prosperity, only partnership in decline and failure.

That might seem harsh, ungrateful, after 300 plus years of being together, of inter-marriage, development of cultural similarities, shedding blood, creating democracy through shared ideas, and building cross-border solidarity in the trade union movement. But the enduring doctrine of state interests requires us to take a cold-blooded look at Scotland's link to England, and conclude that it is no longer good for us to be in a union with it.

It is in our state interests to go. It is in England's state interests to keep us in the union. No matter how pleasant the rhetoric is from English lips about how 'precious' that link is, it is raw English state interests that makes the leaders want to hold us fast. What these state interest are will be addressed later.

Often, we in the independence movement are subject to the patronising line that we are moved by the heart and not by the head. I hope those reading this will see clearly that it is the head and the head alone that is involved here.

Let me temper those harsh realities a little. None of what has gone before will be wasted with a parting of the ways politically. The social union that has been created will continue. Scotland and England will not cease trading. My union Unite (and others) will continue to represent workers in Scotland, England, Wales and all-Ireland as it has done for years. London will remain the great cultural and artistic centre of the British Isles.

There will be a common interest in defence of the island of Great Britain. Scots and English will continue to inter-marry. My anticipated English grandchildren, and present English nieces and nephews will not sever connections with me and other relatives up here – and so it will be for many other families.

But the essentials that determine the fate of a nation – its political and economic sovereignty – require the people of Scotland, whatever their origin, to ignore the sentimental pull of the union heart-strings, apply a hard-headed assessment of our situation within the union, and reach the conclusion that we must leave. The choice before Scotland is either to become poorer along with England, or escape and reconstruct our economy to ensure a prosperous future.

Chapter 2
The English State's Decline

Unionist belief in a big strong UK is false

There are three reasons for optimism. First, desire for independence remains high. Second, the core of support, around 45 per cent, is a solid platform from which to advance. Third, and most important, the case for the Union is growing progressively weaker, and will be weakened ultimately to breaking point.

Quite often one hears people, when complaining of cuts in this or that government programme, proclaiming this should not happen in "one of the richest countries in the world."

The reality, and one Unionists should face, is that the "UK is a poor country pretending to be rich," to quote a headline in The Daily Telegraph. Or as Sherelle Jacobs, right-wing columnist, put it in the same paper on 25.6.24: "Like the middle class, our nation is 'bougie broke'... under the surface, the country is a smoking ruin."

While "smoking ruin" is an overstatement, it captures the despair that is now prevalent in England, and here due to our link to that country. "Poorer Together" in "broken food-bank Britain" in a state "where nothing works" is Scotland's unionist future.

England's condition is not a passing phenomenon. Canute had a better chance of reversing the tide than the

Labour government has of reversing the decline. The UK cannot pay its own way, and each year it is getting worse. The OBR forecast borrowing for 2024-25 as £87bn, then revised the figure to £127bn after Reeves introduced her October 2024 budget, with another later estimate as £137bn. In fact the government in 2024-25 had to borrow £148bn, that is, £148bn more than it took in taxes. The National Debt is now £2.8trn. heading towards £3 trillion. The Office for National Statistics noted in July 2025 that the UK was borrowing £285,000 every minute.

But even those figures don't tell the truth. There are the hidden "off the books" non-accounting of such a magnitude that if all recent Chancellors worked in the private sector, they would be in jail.

The Bank of England, part of the state, is sitting on £179bn of loss from the QE programme. Then there is the £97bn of outstanding PFI debt. But that is dwarfed by the big whopper: the state obligation to pay inflation linked public sector pensions to millions of workers, officially estimated at £1.44trn, to be paid out of current and future taxation. One estimate, taking formally acknowledged national debt and adding the "off the books" numbers, has UK debt liability at £4.38trn.

Economists have described the UK's financial position as a "debt nightmare."

There is no chance of paying down the debt. Instead, bonds have to be issued to roll-over debt, described by the OBR as a "snowball effect." The Debt Management Office is aiming to issue £299.2bn of bonds for financial year 2025-26.The OBR estimate is that debt interest payment will reach £131.6bn a year by 2029-30. Debt interest payment comes before any other expenditure.

Those figures give an accurate picture of a poor country borrowing to pretend to be rich.

*

It was an open secret for many years in Whitehall that the task of the Mandarins at the head of the civil service, along with the elected politicians, was to "manage" the post-imperial decline of the UK. All my adult life, successive governments have struggled and failed to create a successful economy. From 1945 to Thatcher, there was a consistent record of crisis, with the heart of the economy – manufacturing – sinking decade after decade. In the 1959 election Harold Macmillan's Tory boast was that "we had never had it so good." After the war and postwar years of austerity it seemed he was right, but he wasn't. In 1961, two years later, I was a firefighter. We were awarded a pay rise at noon, only to have the Macmillan government cancel it at 2pm as the economy hit the buffers. Tories boast about the great recovery of the Thatcher years but it was less design than luck. The luck of oil taxation revenues pouring into the Treasury: £67.488bn (£200.6 bn at 2021-22 prices) between 1979-1990. The legacy of the Thatcher doctrine was de-industrialisation and mass privatisation of national utilities, a policy that has gone badly with most ending up in foreign ownership.

One negative result of Thatcherism today, of strategic importance, is that while the government is aiming to rebuild the country's military base, with an emphasis on British production, the UK is the only G7 country where a question hangs over its ability to produce the virgin steel needed for its defence industries.

Even before Thatcher was out the door, the normality of economic crisis resumed. Her successor John Major was soon desperately seeking the "green shoots" of recovery from another economic crisis. The Blair government economic policy was dictated by Gordon

Brown as Chancellor. He destroyed the best pension company schemes in the world, spent borrowed money as though it came with no cost and punted new hospital and school building costs "off the books" with PFI, all ending in his final day as Prime Minister with that famous note left in the Treasury drawer: "There is no money." Cameron-Osborne gave us austerity as a method of restoring economic strength, reminiscent of the doctors of old who bled the patient and ended up astonished when death came. Their policy too failed.

A test of an economy's inherent strength is how it deals with and recovers from black swans – that is, unexpected major shocks to the system. As mentioned previously, the UK economy received two: the 2007-08 financial crisis when the banks were saved with austerity and job losses for the people and the Covid pandemic whose mismanagement trashed the economy. Inherent weakness was exposed. The decline that had been evident for years accelerated.

Manufacturing is a case in point. The Tory government of 2019-2024 and the Starmer Labour government claimed growth was their prime aim. But as The Spectator noted (25.1.25): the chemicals industry was down 38 per cent since 2021, cement manufacturing was down 40 per cent, electrical equipment was down 50 per cent, and overall industrial output was down by 10 per cent.

To quote The Spectator, whose editor is Michael Gove: "*This is part of a wider trend of the UK becoming a debtor nation: we do not sell enough goods and services to the rest of the world to keep afloat. The result? We have to tolerate mass foreign ownership of British housing stock, bonds, equities and debt.*"

In short, the UK is living on an international credit card, with those who lend the real masters of the government's economic policies – as Liz Trust quickly found out. Labour's Chancellor is in the same boat, with those who lend demanding a high price as the table below, from 15th June 2025, shows:

10-year bond yields	
UK	4.55%
USA	4.44%
Italy	3.48%
Canada	3.38%
France	3.25%
Germany	2.53%

By 23rd July, the 10-year yield had risen to 4.46%. The 10-year bond yield is the standard measure of the confidence financial markets have of a country's economic ability to repay its debts. There is an additional measure of creditworthiness: the thirty-year bond yield. In July 2025, for the UK, it stood at 5.5%, 1% higher than a year previously.

The US 10-year bond yield is up there with the UK for the same reason: serious questions about debt levels. Donald Trump's Big Beautiful Bill increases the US national debt cap from $36trn to $41trn, to accommodate another $3.4trn of new debt.

A founder of PIMCO, a global investment company with expertise in the bond markets, has made an important policy point about the USA, that is equally applicable to the UK. *If the acquiring of debt to bridge what it earns and what it spends is a temporary measure then there is no long-term problem. But if it is now baked-in government practice to accumulate more and more debt to keep the state operating, a financial crisis is inevitable*. There is, however, a difference between the USA and UK, which postpones the inevitable for the former: the dollar is the world's reserve currency, something that brings with it "an exorbitant privilege" with which the normal rules on debt don't apply. The UK's sterling was, but is no longer, the world's reserve currency.

The Starmer Labour government's first decision (now amended), followed by its first budget, gave us one more version of the truth of decline. That a country claiming to be the sixth biggest economy in the world could not afford to continue paying the winter fuel allowance to pensioners living at the financial edge spoke volumes about the state's finances. Labour's budget, taking taxes to an unprecedented level in peacetime, and ladling on more debt, will prove yet another failure in seeking to reverse the decline. There will be severe political consequences once its failure is fully revealed. We have seen a trailer of what is to come from the 2025 English local elections.

There is another indicator of economic decline which occupies space in the back-business pages of newspapers, but gets hardly a mention on the other media outlets: 700 companies have left the London Stock Exchange, most transferring to Wall Street and thus "leaving the UK as an economic backwater," to quote one economist.

Institutional erosion is there for all to see

But the cause of England's weakened condition goes deeper than is apparent from its economic and social condition. All states rest upon vital institutions and when these erode and are no longer able to support it as before, the rot sets in and compounds other weaknesses.

England's institutional foundations are what I invite Scottish unionists to look at. These are: The Monarchy, Parliament, Civil Service, Political parties, the law (justice and courts), Police, Military, Church of England, BBC, and an intangible element – history as a source of pride and loyalty.

The Monarchy continues to exist, but is weaker as its dysfunctional characters have dispelled the myths. No longer held in reverence, it is now part soap opera, part tragedy, its influence on public life greatly diminished.

Parliament no longer commands the respect that was once axiomatic. Such have been the malpractices over recent years that it now has an independent body monitoring, and effectively being able to unseat MPs. There are few great parliamentarians among its members now.

The Civil Service was once acknowledged worldwide as the Rolls Royce of administration. Not today. It is now best known for covering up failure – the Post Office scandal, the Afghan refugee data leak, Ministry of Defence mismanaging vast sums of money in poor procurement policy, and the Home Office and the Foreign Office where officials block ministerial action, and feel free to issue open letters opposing ministerial policies – not to mention several reforms of the NHS that have compounded its problems.

The law, justice and courts are a mess. At Crown Court level, swift justice for victims of crime no longer exists, nor even early justice. The House of Lords Library noted that 73,105 trials that should have been held did not take place in 2024, with victims of serious crimes such as rape wating four years or more for a trial. Respect and belief in the law as the instrument of justice and safety for the citizen is now problematical for many. It is not only from the Right you hear the cry of two-tier justice.

Police: A look back in time and a view of the present shows how this institution has fallen. A television station shows old films from the 1930s through to the early 1960s. Scotland Yard, the Metropolitan Police, figures in many of them. It is frequently described with absolute confidence as the gold standard of policing. Whether that was once true or not, the MET, the key police institution, was held in high esteem by people in all of the UK.

The opposite is true today. It has been corrupt and, given the criminal conduct of some of its officers, the essential level of trust between it and the public has gone, however unfair that may be to the majority who serve in it. It is in permanent crisis.

It is not only at the Met we see a drop in public estimation. Chief Constables in two other forces are among the hundreds of officers barred from serving.

Military: The navy, army and air force are shadows of their former selves. The navy has two aircraft carriers, and nineteen other warships, frigates and destroyers, of the type needed to form the protective screen around them. Not all ships are operational all the time. There are not enough of them to provide the anti-submarine and anti-aircraft cover that the two carriers require to make them both operational at the same time. The navy can only sail one such group, and even that one is short of the full complement of F35 aircraft. In late September 2024, none of the attack submarines were at sea. It has another problem: it does not have enough sailors.

The army has been so neglected that it would be hard pushed to contribute one division to any war situation.

It is short of its target complement of soldiers. One-tenth of its personnel are not British citizens. A Labour Minister has admitted that the army in its present condition would get destroyed in 'six months to a year' of war. In *Exercise Cerberus* (held in Germany in October 2024), whose purpose was to test the Army's ability to fight large scale battles, there was severe criticism from within its ranks at the poor equipment, with soldiers citing as an example the sixty-year-old Bulldog armoured vehicles breaking down.

The Royal Air Force now lacks capabilities across combat, air transport and early warning aircraft – a condition expected to continue into the 2030s.

Smoke and mirrors: a weak British state pretending to be powerful

The British military was once a Tier 1 force by international standards. UK Governments continue to insist it remains at that status. It isn't true. Looking at the weaponry being used in the war now waged in Europe, few realise that the UK's defence against the kind of missiles Russia is using are the six Type-45 destroyers of the Royal Navy which have anti-missile defence systems. As Group Captain Michael Norris pointed out in a letter to the Times (23.6.25), one is attached to a carrier, others are in for re-fit and therefore not available, and in any case, "ship-based systems are insufficient to defend the entire nation." To this unhappy picture was added, on the eleventh of July, the National Audit Office report that the F-35 warplanes were only able to fly a third of their missions because of shortages of spare parts and engineers.

We are asked to believe that the 2025 Defence Review and the commitment to spend 5% of GDP on "national security" by 2035 will restore the armed forces to the necessary level of lethal power that will cement them in a Tier 1 category. The year 2035 is conveniently ten years away. The term "national security" is elastic and can embrace building civil infrastructure as well as spend on weapons. The only firm commitment from the Labour Government is to up UK defence expenditure from 2.3% to 2.6% of GDP by 2027.

Much vaunted in the spin that accompanied the defence review was the announcement of the intended purchase of twelve F-35A fighter jets from the USA, each capable of delivering twelve intermediate-yield nuclear bombs. Each jet costs around $89m, so a good chunk of that extra 0.3% will go on the aircraft and their weapon, the actual bombs, that the UK does not control.

An American publication gave more valuable information than the UK Labour government did to the people here. The F-35A needs to be refuelled air-to-air by a tanker using a boom – a tube-like device. The RAF has only one tanker, but it uses a drogue, not compatible with a boom, and so cannot refuel. The British F35As will have to rely on the USA tankers.

But that technical hitch pales into insignificance when it is revealed that the bombs carried by each jet will be US made, and, to quote from a report from Chatham House: "Authorisation for using US bombs would rest with the US president, rendering it a far from sovereign capability."

Church of England: This is an English state organisation, whose head is the King, and which as a House of Commons briefing paper noted, "requires parliamentary oversight of its measures." Two of its

Archbishops and twenty-four Bishops sit, as of right now, in the House of Lords and are entitled to take part in debates and votes. Once upon a time, it exercised major influence on government and the people of England. There was a high attendance at its churches on Sundays. Neither is true today. It seems to have lost its theological way, which was never its strong point in any case, with church attendances plunging year after year – 950,000 in the year 2000, to 569,000 in 2022, with only a slight upward attendance among the young. It is riddled with historic scandal.

The Church of Scotland too is in poor shape. But neither it, nor the Church of England, nor the Catholic Church, are the only measures of the strength of Christianity. The Baptist churches, among others not regarded as institutions, are heaving with new worshipers.

BBC: This too is a state institution, whose funding comes from citizens who own a television – the level of which per owner is determined by the state. It once had a monopoly in radio broadcasting and television, a position which gave it great influence in society. Even when that monopoly was broken, the BBC continued to be influential and given almost automatic respect and trust.

That is no longer the case. It is regarded by many, on the Right and Left, as run by a metropolitan elite living in a self-constructed bubble and unable to understand or comprehend the lives of the people it is supposed to serve. Its influence is waning by the year.

The Political Parties: Tory and Labour have been the political institution of the English state since 1945, each taking it in turns to govern. They have been at the tiller as the ship has floundered. Both have shed membership numbers at scale. Voter turnout has markedly declined, a measure of people's lack of confidence in them, and slid to a low of 60 per cent in 2024, producing a government elected on only 33 per cent of those voting, or put another way, supported by only 25 per cent of the total entitled to vote.

Between 2007 and 2024 the UK has had five prime ministers – Brown, Cameron, May, Johnston and Sunak, leaving no trace of any great accomplishments, with each leaving the successor with problems magnified.

As is usually the case when a society finds its "normality" not working, it looks for a quick fix, a magical solution. Step forward Reform, born in England and wrapped round the single personality of a quintessential English Nationalist: Nigel Farage. He is able to capitalise on the sense of betrayal and hopelessness that is a mark of UK life, and he plays well to the gallery of anger in England. But his policy statements, more police on the streets, imposition of law and order, longer prison sentences, are orthodox right-wing. If he were alive, Norman Tebbit would have no difficulty in singing from the same hymn sheet. Nigel Farage, no more than the other political party leader, does not understand the deep historical and structural reasons for his country's decline.

That Reform should also be here in Scotland is consistent with the fact that we, as part of the UK, share in its decline and many of our people share in the sense of hopelessness that is now part and parcel of life as a UK citizen.

"Each civilisation dies from indifference towards
the unique values which created it"
Nicolas Gomes D'Avilla

Each of the pillars the English state has rested upon are crumbling. But there is another factor in its decline, not material or physical but vital to any nation: pride among its people in what it is and where it came from. That pride was once unquestioned. But not now. Intellectual self-flagellation based on a repudiation of England's history is a marked feature of its elite in the universities, among their graduates, and in many of its institutions and major civic organisations. Polls say that half of Generation Z believe the UK is racist, and only 11 per cent would be willing to fight for it in a war. The willingness of so many English people to cloak themselves in the guilt of their ancestors, who themselves felt no guilt over the empire and slave trade, has turned previous national heroes into pariahs.

As each icon of the past has been knocked down, the ground on which previous generations of the English felt pride in their national history has been undermined, and national self-respect and self-confidence sapped.

Nothing illustrates this better than the decision of the Shakespeare Birthplace Trust to "decolonialise his legacy" and "purge" the SBT of "Anglo-centric and colonialist thought" because of "the role Shakespeare has been forced to play in establishing and upholding imperialist narratives of cultural supremacy."

Shakespeare (1564-1616) wrote when England controlled virtually nothing but England, with the Empire still to come. If – as the Trust has claimed – Shakespeare's legacy "promotes white supremacy" and "imperialist narratives of cultural supremacy," why would James Baldwin, renowned African-American author and civil rights activist, express his admiration for the "greatness" of the Bard? Why, if Shakespeare is such a potential villain did Rabindranath Tagore, the first non-European to win the Nobel Prize in literature, and one of the founders of the Indian independence movement, write a poem in celebration of Shakespeare's works reaching the "palm groves by the Indian sea"?

It is as though England of the past was unique in its subjugation of other peoples in building its empire, in enslaving and selling people, and therefore a nation damned with a permanent moral guilt. No other nation in the twenty-first century quite reaches the same level of contempt for its past as the English do.

Islam today glides over the fact that the Prophet Muhammed had slaves, as did the Muslim empires that were built upon his new religion. The Koran accommodates slavery, but insisted that slaves were human beings, banned their mistreatment, and saw them being granted freedom as a virtue. No one was ever held as a chattel slave. There was an interesting twist to Islamic slave policy: Muslims were prohibited from enslaving Muslims, and others could only be enslaved if bought or taken in war.

The benefit of asserting slaves as human beings can be seen in the practices of the great Muslim empire, that of the Ottomans. Slaves could rise to the highest offices, and other slaves such as the Janissaries formed the standing army of the Sultan and came to play, on occasion, a decisive role in who became the Sultan.

No such modification of slavery existed for the Christian African slave traders, and those in the Caribbean and the United States who bought and used them. They traded in humans as sub-human property. There must have been in all the years of the Atlantic trade brilliant Africans who, if the Muslim system of acknowledging them as human beings had been practiced, would have made a far greater contribution to Caribbean and Southern state societies than picking cotton.

Present day African leaders don't shirk their ancestors' complicity in the trade, but they are sensible in addressing historic actions they cannot reverse. In Benin, Cameroon, Ghana, and Nigeria, leaders have all made apologies. Luc Gnacadja's apology on behalf of Benin was clear: "We cry for forgiveness and reconciliation. The slave trade is a shame and we repent it." In Cameroon, a formal apology was made to an American descendent of slaves for the Oku clan's historic selling of his ancestors and other captives into slavery. In Ghana, in 2022, Nanas Obokese Ampah I, the traditional King of Asebu, issued this apology: "It is time to address what must be said to the African Diaspora. We must engage in a meaningful conversation to acknowledge and reconcile our actions and inactions as rulers of our kingdoms during the Trans-Atlantic Slave Trade, which we deeply regret."

That's it from Africa. Ancestors engaging in slavery acknowledged. No expectation of being morally bound to make reparations to African-Americans, Caribbeans or others whose ancestors were sent west. They seem able to see their ancestors as people of their time, very different from ours, something the English seem unable to do. They seem unable, because of the guilt of slave trading, to celebrate that it was England principally – given the dominance of that component in parliament – that was the first to abolish slavery in its own domains but also sought to eradicate it wherever the Royal Navy could establish control.

The English empire, with enthusiastic Scottish involvement, did what all empires do – create among its people a sense of right to rule others, and be certain of superiority over those conquered and occupied. The Romans, Persians, Spanish, Portuguese, Chinese, Ottomans all saw themselves as superior to others, and often put that forward to justify their empires.

Scotland, as I have alluded to above, was woven into the English empire, with keen participation in the slave trade, and the exploitation of enslaved Africans in the Caribbean. The book *Bought & Sold: Scotland, Jamaica and Slavery* lays out the profitable Scottish involvement in chattel slavery and the inhumane treatment that went with it.

Efforts have been made to make present day Scots face up to what our ancestors did in imperial days. The slave traders were at the top of the social hierarchy with working class soldiers in the military dishing out death while being as racist in their beliefs as the officers who commanded them. That racism was still there, a long timer later, at both ends of the social scale as I found when joining the Royal Navy in the 1950s. Egyptians and other Arabs were "Wogs," Chinese "Chinkies," and Black people disparaged.

There is validity in the argument that we should not judge people by the moral standards of our times, but see them in their times when their practices were regarded as the norm. But if that is wholly valid, then those times would never have changed. They changed because even in those times there were men and women who saw the immorality inherent in the norms, openly called them immoral, and campaigned to remove them.

There has not in Scotland, however, been the same readiness to self-flagellate about the Empire and its attendant crimes as is observable in England. Perhaps we have been able to slide into the shadow offered by being the junior partner.

The handling of Robert Burns is instructive. There were early attempts to place him in the dungeon of sin, but these came to nothing. Most Scots weren't having our Rabbie belittled and his statues defaced. When Edinburgh University – in that first flush of wokery – removed the name of Hume from one of its buildings, it was far from universally applauded, with some asking if his name was taboo, why did the university still teach his philosophy? His statue still sits prominently in the Lawnmarket near St. Giles.

We have had token gestures. Edinburgh City Council appointed the late Professor Sir Geoff Palmer to review the statues and street names in the city, but no statutes have come down, no streets re-named. Even Dundas still stands on his plinth, albeit with a plaque recording his intransigence over the efforts to abolish slavery. Its accuracy has been contested by Scottish historians such as Michel Fry and Tom Devine, with the latter accused of being a racist by Professor Palmer. An accusation we all know is absurd.

But there is a legacy impressed upon modern times from the Atlantic slave trade

The empire was, in its essentials, the exploitation by the British state, and the actors engaged on its behalf, of the territory and peoples it subjugated and ruled. It was accompanied by brutality and atrocity, with both rooted in a belief of racial superiority. Democratic countries have proved no different from authoritarian ones in maintaining occupation by force. The United States' suppression of the Huks in the Philippines, Britain's at Amritsar and the Hola death camp in Kenya are examples. "Good" things were done that were long lasting, like the idea of the rule of law, the introduction of modern medicines, and infrastructure, but these were done primarily to make the occupation more effective and profitable.

The English, Scots, and Irish, had a majority that were people of their time for whom creating an empire was a legitimate objective, with slavery a natural commercial trade as it had been for centuries in all parts of the world where humans built their societies – there were five tribes in North America who had slaves. There was the longstanding Trans-Saharan slave trade, Red Sea, Indian Ocean and Atlantic trade. The only white involvement was in the Atlantic trade. Slavery was catered for in the Bible (Exodus 21:2) and Islamic law.

Its widespread practice from the first organised societies in antiquity to the 19th century saw that no civilisation was free from its presence.

But the Atlantic slave trade was in one unique respect different from the others at that time, and beforehand. It was the first time in the history of slavery that colour became a dominant factor in how enslaved people were seen, and treated. In the Caribbean and America, white people regarded black slaves as less then human, and so could impose upon them the appalling conditions onboard the slave ships, and inhumane treatment in the plantations. A "subordinate and inferior class of beings" was how United States Chief Justice Taney described black slaves in the infamous Dred Scott judgement in 1857. A slave was counted as three-fifths of a white in the American calculations for the voting rights of its states' representation in Congress.

It is little wonder that racist attitudes still exist in British society (and in the USA). I am a child of the empire, born in 1937 with it being still intact. On our primary school class wall was a huge map with the empire painted in red. Our teachers explained that it was "ours", an empire upon which the Sun never set. The general message from the classroom, newspapers and politicians was that the empire was a good thing, with us teaching and governing other people not yet able to govern themselves. That was widely accepted as true.

Implicit in the imperial message was that we were superior, and that superiority had to be protected. Even in sport. The British Boxing Council operated a colour bar until 1948, barring any British-born coloured boxer from fighting for the national professional championships. I remember, at around ten years of age, listening to a BBC wireless commentary on a fight in which one boxer was superior to his opponent, and being astounded when one commentator said to the other that it was a pity the winner could not fight for the British title as, although he was born in Britain, he was prevented by "the colour bar."

It takes a long time for attitudes like that, deeply embedded, to be eradicated.

Prejudice against people of colour still exists in western society, despite laws and the emergence of changing attitudes especially among the young. It is a living malignant legacy straight from the Atlantic trade in people whose skins were black. What happened to their ancestors is a present pain to a great many people of colour in Britain and the former colonies; it is evident that many of them remain convinced that the Taney view of them still operates in their interaction with western state institutions, and society in general.

For those in the former colonies, there is an understandable desire to "get even" for the historical injustice done when the slave owners received compensation for the loss of their human property (**£20m then** equal to £1.7bn now) while the slaves got nothing. Their cry for reparations should not be brushed aside, but neither should white citizens of the UK cave in to it as though we alone are guilty, and so we alone should pay a financial penalty.

*

What we can do is tackle that lingering legacy of racism with consistency and, whilst acknowledging that its strain is still evident, build upon the progress that has been made. That Humza Yousaf could become First Minister, Anas Sarwar lead the Labour party in Scotland, Rishi Sunak could become prime minister, and Kemi Badenoch succeed him as leader of a major party, with very few thinking it unusual is a mark of the progress we have made. The few who did make a big thing of Kemi Badenoch's appointment were, paradoxically, themselves black.

If payment of reparation via cash is unjustified and impossible, it does not mean we in the UK should brush aside the Caribbean view with its roots in historical injustice. That historical injustice to their ancestors, the transfer of wealth they produced to enrich white families, banks and financial institutions here, was a distinctive advantage to the British state's investment in and management of the industrial revolution, giving us a scientific and technological lead that, compared with Caribbean development, we have never lost.

We should acknowledge that, and seek actively and organisationally to partner with the Caribbean by twinning the West Indies University, with designated Russell Group universities' science and engineering departments, along with fully paid scholarships for Masters and PhD students. Russell Group universities have access to resources in the sciences and technology that the West Indies University does not have.

A final point: one of the ironies of the Taney judgement in the USA, and the belief of white supremacists today is that far from being inferior, Africans and their descendants are the only holders of 100 per cent DNA of the human species. Whites in the northern regions have at least 2 per cent of Neanderthal DNA, while those in the Southern region have around 2 per cent of Denisovan DNA. The reason is that those who stayed in Africa did not meet and have intercourse with others in the human branches.

Chapter 3
Addressing our unionist fellow citizens – I was one too

Without converting a key percentage of today's unionists, we cannot win independence. Getting them to listen is essential if we are to persuade them towards a change of mind, and that can only come with a change of attitude towards them. In short, civilised dialogue not foul-mouthed insults.

Before we start to ask them to listen, we in the movement need to recognise that it is legitimate to be a unionist. That is the first step to what is indispensable for successful persuasion – respect. To accomplish the aim of conversion, we need to start with what has been missing: a serious attempt to understand why they are unionist.

Unionists are not anti-Scottish. They have a genuine concern for the Scotland they live in. They have honestly believed it is better for us to stay within a strong UK. Our task is to persuade them of the truth: that such belief is now demonstrably false and that being so it requires people like them, deeply concerned and committed to making Scotland a better place, to think again about independence, and the Scottish society that can be created by it with their involvement.

Before independence activists start engaging with our unionist colleagues (I hope) it may help them to that understanding if I cite my own journey from being a unionist, elected as such as a Labour MP in 1970, to a conversion making me an advocate for independence. There was no road to Damascus. It was a slow burn from one to the other.

I went to the Westminster parliament in full favour of the union. For me, who had been an official at the Scottish TUC, the UK government's industrial policy of constraining investment projects in the successful English areas like the Midlands, matched by incentives to attract new development to the North East of England and Scotland, was in Scotland's interests, and therefore my country was being well served by its place in the union.

But within two years as an MP, at the centre of UK government, with more sources of information than the ordinary citizen could have, or even a senior STUC official had available, I began to have doubts, coming from a combination of matters I was able to observe.

There was the one day in summer when we Scots MPs had the House of Commons to ourselves to debate the Scottish economy, on a motion tabled by the government, amended by the opposition, and therefore voted upon. I realised that this was not a mark of our importance, but a great convenience for those English toffs who wanted to attend one of the major horse race events, and for other MPs to have a day off. We had a Labour majority of Scottish MPs but at 10pm, when the vote was called, we were swamped by the English Tories coming in for a few minutes to vote down our motion or amendment. I saw it as farcical, but revealing of the true nature of the British state, in which Scottish interests were accorded only token recognition.

Then there were the committees that dealt in detail with Scottish Bills. The government Tory side, because they had fewer Scottish MPs, brought in English MPs to make up their numbers, who sat silent but voted down our amendments. Winning a majority in Scotland produced impotence instead of power.

One of the most important influences in my development was a recognition of the imperial hangover, the grand illusion that the UK was still a great power, which applied to both Tory and Labour parties. This illusion had damaging practical effects on economic policy, with resources that should have been invested in the domestic economy allocated to maintaining overseas military commitments which were obviously beyond the state's ability to sustain. This was especially so as the 1960s and 70s saw the country enter another long period of economic crisis. How my country of Scotland could prosper in that scenario was a serious question for me to answer.

*

I began to doubt if the Westminster unionist construct could deliver the kind of policies that were required to lift Scots to the economic and social level that I wanted for us. If the union as it then was constructed didn't work for Scots, what might?

So, I sat down and argued with myself, and did so by writing a thirteen-page personal memo exploring the pros and cons of Scottish self-government. At first, given that I had made my name as the hammer of the Nats, I was not inclined to embrace independence, so it was the "safe" position of devolution that I found most attractive. But once out of the trench of a unionist mind, I came over time to realise that devolution doesn't fundamentally change the power relationship between the centre and the minority areas of a unitary state.

As Enoch Powell put it bluntly, devolution is "power retained" at Westminster. Notwithstanding that fact, I came to understand also that in such a lopsided union, the interests of the large component – England – would always by necessity dictate economic policy.

This was brought home to me by the actions of the Midlands Labour MPs group, who had set out to kill off the "levelling up" industrial policy. The UK had entered yet another economic crisis and unemployment was rising in the Midlands as well as elsewhere. I watched as through well organised and targeted questions and speeches that were both written and oral, the Midlands group put pressure on the government to abandon the "levelling up" industrial policy.

I met some of them to complain about what they were doing, as it meant the advantage Scotland was supposed to get was being eliminated. I still remember the brutal answer along the lines of "you might put up with unemployment; we won't and if that means the end of this policy then so be it." For them, the Midlands, a key area of England, was what mattered. It was an expression of English national interest.

There was another phenomenon I found as I moved to devolution. Once out of the unionist mentality of everything having to come from the central government in London, I could think of doing things differently, but then I hit the wall of limited powers that is devolution, especially in the economic policy areas.

Oil was the best example. It was in Scotland's interest to have a slow start to the exploitation of the North Sea, so that like Norway we could build up a genuine oil industry throughout the country and replace the old industries with a new one. That meant not only the construction side of the industry, but also research and development. The North Sea, a turbulent one, presented challenges to this global industry. New extraction technology was needed, but that actually took place elsewhere, mainly in Texas.

A slower start to the development of extraction and time to build a new all-encompassing oil industry was the best policy for Scotland, but not the United Kingdom which needed it to flow in large volume to bring much needed revenue into the Treasury, and also help with the balance of payments between what we exported and imported – a factor that has plagued all UK governments since 1945.

I recall attending a meeting in the early 1970s between the head of an oil company and a group of Labour MPs where the former, advocating swift and extensive development of the North Sea was particularly vehement about the Norwegians who would not play along with him and the other oil majors. He called the Norwegians the "blue-eyed Arabs."

*

As the government's economic policies morphed into crisis, I started to question whether my belief in the UK's ability to deliver better times for the people I came from was valid.

For the first time in my life the Scottish national interest started to emerge as a concept. Few Scots thought in those terms and regrettably that is still the case. "National interests" when spoken about by British statesmen was about English national interests. We Scots have not thought about ours for more than 300 years.

It was when I fully grasped the importance of seeing things in terms of Scottish national interests, and saw how often they were pushed aside for the national interests of the big nation, that I came to see the reality: the United Kingdom is a fiction – it is England with a Scottish subordinate appendage. That final understanding took me eventually from devolution, a solution within the UK, to independence.

But before I was anywhere near to embracing independence, I still could not fully divorce myself from the unionist belief that had been my compass for so many years. I opted for "powerful" devolution, as the best of both worlds – still in the UK but a Scotland with different possibilities. Writing now in 2025, that 1970s idea of mine seems tame and woefully inadequate. I saw "powerful" as giving a Scottish Assembly, not a parliament, full powers over the Scottish Development Agency, and being able to tinker with employment laws.

Having invested so much of my belief in the union, and given the pull it had on me because of my affinity with others south of the border politically, as a socialist trade unionist, I found it intellectually and emotionally difficult to reject the union in favour of independence and it took time to do so.

It will be the same journey for those unionists who begin to see the UK for what it has become, weakened and in decline, and start to consider a change of mind on independence. To make that transfer of belief a faster one than mine, respect and understanding has to lie at the heart of the debate and dialogue we must have with them.

Chapter 4
Why Scotland matters to England

We are back at 1707

Always at the forefront of our minds when making policy should be reality that dictates all international relations: geography, spheres of influence and state interests. Those factors have been a constant ever since the Amarna Age (1500-1100 B.C.E) covering much of the region we know as the Middle East, which scholars identify as the start of international relations.

Taking account of those three realities will assist us in understanding why there is a great deal at stake for England in Scottish independence – and also for certain others.

In this book I sometimes refer to the UK as England. They are interchangeable, because England is eighty-five per cent of the UK population, and that fact has led to it being the dominant part of the UK in domestic, foreign and defence policy since the union was formed. It is no accident or slip of the tongue that "England" is how the UK was described both here and abroad for a long time, and still frequently is. I don't use "England" in any sense of resentment when I use it for the UK. It is the reality.

Although the words United Kingdom refers to the British state, it is the Scottish-English relationship that is at the heart of it. This is spelled out in plain language in Schedule 5, Reserved matters, The Constitution, Part I, 1(b) of the Scotland Act 1998 which refers to: "the Union of the Kingdoms of Scotland and England."

Look at the different attitude England takes towards Northern Ireland and Scotland. When Prime Ministers and other Ministers declare their love for "this precious Union," it is not true if they mean what at present constitutes the United Kingdom.

England, the Kingdom of which includes the principality of Wales, does not think it would be threatened by the departure of Northern Ireland. Indeed, both in the 1998 Good Friday Agreement and the Northern Ireland Act 1998, there is specific provision made for Northern Ireland to depart and join the Republic of Ireland if a majority wishes to do so.

The Good Friday Agreement states that the signatories, which includes the UK government, "recognise that it is for the people of the island of Ireland *alone*, by agreement between the two parts respectively and *without external impediment*, to exercise their right of self-determination on the basis of consent, freely and concurrently given, North and South, to bring about a united Ireland, if that is their wish, accepting that this right must be achieved and exercised with and subject to the agreement and consent of a majority of the people of Northern Ireland." (emphasis added)

The Northern Ireland Act 1998, giving effect to that agreement, makes specific provision by Order in Council, for the UK secretary of state to trigger a border poll enabling the people of that part of the UK to leave it. The part I have highlighted in the agreement, ensures that the UK government will have no role in the debate leading to a decision. There will be no UK government "project fear" aimed at Northern Ireland's people or any other involvement on the unionist side of that referendum campaign.

In the Brexit debates, Ian Blackford MP, SNP parliamentary leader, pointed to the special status of Northern Ireland in the EU Withdrawal Agreement and asked why no such similar arrangement is being applied to Scotland. The answer is simple: England's national interests. England would not be unhappy to see Northern Ireland depart and join the Republic. I cannot think of any other country today that would, as the UK has done with Northern Ireland, voluntarily place part of its territory within the economy of a foreign power (in this case the EU) when previously it was fully integrated in the UK. That Brexit consequential, taken together with the terms, and implications, of the Good Friday Agreement, contains the message "we don't care if you go." The Ulster Unionists get it, as do the Nationalists.

The difference between Westminster's policy towards Northern Ireland and Scotland, is that the former is of no strategic importance to England, whereas Scotland is. We are seeing history repeat itself.

In 1707, England needed to take us into the Union. Think what Scottish independence means for England. Another state on this island, with its own different state interests, in a geographical position of strategic importance for England's security, and a border on this island for the first time in over 300 years. That is not something the English state will welcome. It is something other states, with state interests of their own, will have a view on too.

Why Scotland in the Union is a Strategic Necessity for England: the Unsinkable Aircraft Carrier

Today, again for England, the retention of Scotland is strategically a national interest, both in defence and foreign policy. It is no coincidence that over a number of weeks in June 2021, with independence still dominating the agenda, articles began to appear by columnists in the English press, along with a statement by Ben Wallace the then defence secretary of state, about how "security" of the whole UK was a factor to consider in the context of Scottish independence.

This was a new "Scottish" slant on foreign and defence policy, as over the past 300 years Scotland has been seen in that context, not as a problem, but an asset to security.

Our Scottish press has foreign news pages, but that is not the same as people within the nation, or our elected politicians, producing in-depth papers and articles on a wide range of international issues, or our political parties debating foreign policy at their conferences. How could we expect that when the Labour and Tory parties in Scotland are not autonomous, but mere branches of UK parents, which expect no more of them than concentration on domestic affairs? While the SNP has been obsessed with gender, grievance with any government that sits in Westminster, and its love affair with Brussels.

It is only in 2022 that a foreign policy think tank has been created in Scotland by a number of academics. I doubt if many people know about it as of yet.

It is only in the London based newspapers, journals and think-tanks that discussion and debates on foreign policy have been held. This a blind spot in the independence movement, carrying a failure to recognise how important England sees us in the context of its position in the world's institutions. We have to open Scottish eyes to why England has sound strategic reason to hold on to us. Because that is why it will fight a fierce political battle, no holds barred, to keep us.

Our eyes must also be open to the interests of other powers who share the English view about our strategic location, and make sure we do not make adversaries or enemies out of them, to the point where they may feel it necessary to intervene against us, in subtle if not open ways. The movement should now form an international relations policy designed to make other powers who may be affected by independence supportive (unlikely), or neutral (which would be a plus).

Such a policy is not easy to formulate given the stances taken by most parts of the movement, with criticism of the United States, NATO, and nuclear weapons. Up to now we have acted in protest mode (me too). But to achieve independence we have to start thinking in state terms, recognising our geographical importance, and assessing other states' interests about which we shall have to consider.

We are a small nation seeking independence, a matter on which other, larger states, and alliances of states, will have views, and perhaps influence. When acting as a protest movement we have the luxury of being righteous. A serious movement which aims to lead a small nation to gain its aim, has to accommodate realities it will find uncomfortable.

*

So, why does Scotland matter to England primarily (and to others)? Two areas have always been regarded as vital: defence and foreign policy. Both have been accentuated since the rise of China as a major power and by the Russian invasion of Ukraine. England's defence is linked to NATO's requirement of a steady supply of materials and armed forces from North America via the Atlantic to Europe. Scotland is vital to England's defence, and in respect of influence on the world, shorn of Scotland, England would be an even more diminished figure in the international arena than now.

Trump's policy has raised questions about a long-term American commitment to NATO. There are influential people within his administration, and outside his group of Republican advisers, who see US interests as being in the Asia-Pacific, with Europe relegated as peripheral. If NATO becomes primarily a European organisation or the EU and UK construct a new defence system, nothing will change in Scotland's strategic importance.

How England views Scotland in its defence policy cannot be overstated. It is too narrow a definition of "defence" to think of it only in terms of preventing or defeating an invasion of this island. Cyber warfare is a new dimension in defence calculations of course, but some things do not change – the vulnerability of this island which relies heavily on importing materials and food for its existence, with much of it coming from north America via the Atlantic.

Today's admirals are as blindly devoted to the aircraft carrier as the pre-1939 ones were to the battleship. Gordon Brown committed billions of pounds to building two of them, which a number of defence specialists regard as white elephants. The only carrier that has been attacked since 1945 is the US one targeted by the Yemeni Houthis in the Red Sea in 2025. The Houthi weapons have been easily dealt with. The real question for the future is whether carriers would survive rockets arriving at some several thousands of miles an hour, like the ones being developed by a new sea power such as China.

A secure location enabling interdiction of an enemy's ability to disrupt a vital supply link is where Scotland comes into the English and NATO picture. Unlike an aircraft carrier, Scotland is unsinkable. Air power launched from Scotland, along with submarines based at Faslane, can close the Iceland and other gaps, thus denying an adversary access to the Atlantic from the North Sea. It was Scotland's importance to UK defence, and integration into NATO, that motivated *The Economist* to devote pages of analysis in its 5th November 2020 edition, under the heading "How Scottish Independence would threaten Britain's defence."

The role, position and possible fate of the Trident nuclear weapon submarine base at Faslane figured prominently, as did the fact that it is also the UK's non-nuclear-weaponed submarine base. However, equal weight was devoted to the RAF's ability to interdict enemy submarines or warships transiting from the North Sea through the Iceland gaps and Denmark Strait into the Atlantic to attack convoys.

The SNP's decision that Scotland should join NATO still leaves policy swimming through muddy waters, as it has not repudiated its absolute opposition to any part of Scotland hosting nuclear weapons. But as *The Economist* points out, "NATO is a self-proclaimed 'nuclear alliance,' and America, which routinely uses Faslane, does not tell allies when nuclear-armed planes or ships are passing through allied territory." Thrown into the pot by *The Economist*'s analysis was the cost of relocating Trident – £3-4bn, something that would take years. That relocation cost is by now much higher.

It is so long since Scotland was a nation state that held debates about state interests and spheres of influence, it is little wonder they do not figure into our internal political life to any great extent. Outside of our universities, it is rare to hear arguments between the realist and idealist schools of foreign policy. Yet we do live in a world where state interests and spheres of influence are what matter. In or out of the UK, Scotland is well and truly embedded in the United States' sphere of influence. Scotland is also in the sphere of influence and within the states' interests of the western EU NATO countries.

Scotland will feel the pressure of that reality when we come within touching distance of independence and we shall feel its full force if we become independent.

I speak from experience. In the 1970s Billy Wolfe, leader of the SNP, visited the US State Department. Asked about Polaris, the nuclear weapon system (now replaced by Trident), he told them it would be out pronto on independence. By coincidence, along with Neil Kinnock (both of us Labour MPs), I was in the State Department a few weeks later and was immediately informed of Billy's statement. They took it seriously.

During the 1979 referendum on whether Scotland would have a Scottish Assembly (a mild form of devolution), the US Consul General in Edinburgh was a former CIA agent who left immediately after the referendum failed. During the campaign and up to referendum polling day, CIA agents were regular visitors to Scotland. They didn't hide their identities or interests and they met politicians openly. Before the vote, and bear in mind this was about an Assembly with no powers regarding defence, the US Ambassador came to Scotland and openly opposed devolution. He met Margo MacDonald and I and the matter he raised was Polaris. The US State Department took the "slippery slope" argument – from devolution to independence – seriously. It is unlikely that the US view of the importance of Scotland has changed. In formulating a comprehensive policy for independence, which means taking account of the powerful interests of others, difficulties will be faced on whether to maintain old positions, on Trident for example, or compromise them to accommodate the interests of others.

I can recall delegates at an SNP conference giving thunderous applause to Willie Slaven when quoting Charles Stewart Parnell, he cried "No man has the right to fix the boundaries of a nation." Brilliant rhetoric, but not true. Depending on its geography and importance to other greater powers, a small nation has to live with limitations. That is particularly so when a small nation still has yet to achieve sovereignty.

The Arctic: a new geopolitical reality making Scotland important to others

The Arctic has now, due to a warmer earth, become a geopolitical strategic area on par with the Atlantic and Pacific oceans in the security and economic life of the United States, EU, Russia and China. There is still ice to be broken as ships go through, but what was previously impassible for commercial vessels is no longer so in some parts. To quote The Economist of 25th January 2025: "A warming Arctic should yield enormous dividends.

Retreating ice will create shipping shortcuts. Maritime access and melting glaciers will make it easier to extract minerals, just when the world craves resources from the Arctic's virgin geology." A RUSI paper from the 15th April 2025 estimates that shipping through the Arctic can "slash travel times between Asia and Europe by up to 40%."

A look at the map shows why for both security and economic reasons Donald Trump wanted Greenland, and although Scotland's proximity to the Arctic comes nowhere near that of Greenland, we are in a crucial place in respect of sea lanes leading to it from the south and the North Sea. As the Arctic becomes of ever greater importance, our geography embeds Scotland further into the spheres of influence and state interests of the United States and NATO.

This is made plain in that RUSI paper: "The trajectory of Arctic security is not a distant concern for Britain – it is a direct vulnerability. If Russia's Northern Fleet were to tighten control over the Greenland-Iceland-UK (GIUK) Gap, the Royal Navy would face a strategic chokepoint that could sever transatlantic supply lines. This is not just a hypothetical risk: the Royal Navy has confirmed increased Russian patrols near UK waters, underscoring the Arctic's role as a gateway to the UK itself." Those UK waters are not the English Channel but North Sea and Atlantic waters around Scotland.

The RUSI conclusion is that "The Royal Navy should establish year-round Arctic-ready patrol capabilities – not only to support NATO partners but to ensure Britain's own freedom of navigation." And where would be the best location for the bases for this new component of naval presence? Scotland is the obvious answer.

The other strategic (political) reason Scotland matters to England The United Nations Security Council seat

The five United Nations Security Council permanent members' seats, carrying veto power over resolutions, were conceived in recognition of the then Great Powers in the world of 1945. There were actually only three great powers: USA, USSR and UK, but Roosevelt insisted to include China despite it being in a bad way, with Churchill arguing successfully to include France although contrary to what de Gaulle claimed, it had to be liberated by the UK and USA.

Today only the USA and China are Great Powers. Russia gives itself the belief it is still one of them, but its special relationship with China is more akin that of the UK to the USA (a junior partner) than a bond between equals. France if pushed can always claim to be representative of a major region: the EU.

That brings us to England. There is no hiding that it is now a second rank power, yet still sits on the Security Council. Like the other four it is a nuclear power but being such is not a true measurement of where its place now is in the world rankings.

The UK stripped of Scotland would stand exposed as England, holding a UN Security Council seat when others who can mount a greater claim remain excluded. Those others include Japan, India, Indonesia, Brazil, South Africa, Nigeria, and Turkey - all of whom have either greater global or regional importance than does England.

The five permanent members can make international law, such as the application of sanctions. Their support or non - support is important to other UN states when seeking UN action. The UK being one of them, therefore, has a status, importance, and influence affecting world events unsurpassed by any other second ranking power. Retention of that position is what is at stake for England with Scottish independence.

It is not me who says this. The *Daily Telegraph* reported on the 17th of October 2012, two years before the last referendum, that the "Foreign and Commonwealth Office (FCO)" had predicted to the Foreign Affairs Select Committee that "Hostile foreign leaders would exploit Scottish independence to try and curtail the UK's power on the world stage… It is understood they fear Argentina would try to have the UK removed as one of the five permanent members of the UN security council."

The *Guardian* reported on the 10th of September 2014, the same anxiety this time from former Prime Minister John Major: he "outlined the impact an independent Scotland would have on the standing of the remainder of the UK in the world. He said the UK would lose the Trident nuclear deterrent, which is based in Scotland, and would struggle to keep its permanent seat on the UN Security Council."

That was the view before Brexit, when EU had an interest in sustaining the permanent membership of two of its states – the UK and France. I doubt if that would be the case now with the UK.

Just think for a moment: today because of that UNSC position, the UK prime minister, foreign secretary and diplomatic corps matter in the world. Their support is lobbied for. Their closeness to the United States, a fellow permanent member, means that many beat a path to their doors, using them to gain access to the White House to further their own interests. Divested of that permanent UNSC position, who would bother knocking on the door of Downing Street or the Foreign Office, or listen to lectures from the political leaders of a much reduced second-rate power? England stripped of its UN position would become in the words of Lord Richards, formerly chief of the defence staff: "Belgium with nukes."

In the diplomatic world, losing that UNSC seat would be, for the UK, equivalent to losing a war, with all its consequences of humiliation and terminal loss of authority in the international arena.

There is going to be a great deal at stake for the British state and its Whitehall establishment in the future referendum on Scotland. It is as much about their future too, as it is ours. That is why the way the UK government fights its corner in the next referendum will not be a repeat of 2014 when it was sure it would win, and invented Project Fear, and then the Vow, when it watched the rise of the Yes vote. That applies to whatever party's prime minister sits in 10 Downing Street.

Chapter 5
It all comes down to what is best for the economic life of this nation

There is an economic reason for Independence but we also need to change something in ourselves

Unionists occupy a peculiar position: they admit that an independent Scotland could be viable but also argue that becoming so would be a disaster. The movement, by comparison, is sustained by the belief that independence will bring us success both economically and socially. Before the Covid pandemic, unionists pointed to a budget deficit of £12bn as an insuperable obstacle to independence, threatening the misery of huge cuts in public spending. They are, post-pandemic, as result of the UK Treasury splashing the cash (courtesy of the Bank of England), able to point to a £36bn deficit on a putative Scottish budget.

It is commonplace for unionist criticism of the very idea of independence to point to Scotland as being a heavily subsidised part of the UK, a view endorsed in their eyes by the above-mentioned deficits.

Unionists have never grasped that when they promote the image of a subsidised Scotland, unable to stand on our own economic feet, they are damning not the whole 318 years of union, but the modern section of that period – the post 1945 Scotland within the UK. If after 80 years as an integral part of the British economy, with macro-economic decisions, pre- and post-devolution, made by the British cabinet, Scotland is a subsidised junkie, then the Union system has failed us.

Two of the key measures of economic progress are population growth and emigration. In 1707 Scotland's population was 1m. England's was 3m. In 2025 Scotland's population is around 5.4m whereas England is around 58m. We continue, as was the case after WWII, to export a high proportion of our human talent to England, Canada, Australia and New Zealand. Not a plus for those who see the Union as something we should endorse as successful.

Is there really a Scottish, *Scottish* economy?

I don't here set out in detail a new White Paper, a new post-Brexit, post-pandemic economic policy for an independent Scotland. That is not a task for a single individual. Indeed, charting the course of any economy is going to be a difficult task as the new technological revolution gathers pace. I am, however, setting out principles and concepts, that could make independence a success.

Let me start with that question: is there actually now a Scottish, *Scottish* economy? One that, while influenced by, is not actually controlled by another's macro-economic and monetary policies? No. What we have in Scotland are sectors of activity: the NHS, housing, rail and roads are under the control of a Scottish government operating within a budget over which it does not have a final say. But in terms of "the economy" in the full sense of that word, Scotland is a mere adjunct of the large dominant English one south of our borders

– where lies the power of the Treasury and other UK government departments with their macro-economic levers, including a central bank whose Governor, Board and Monetary Policy Committee exercise decisive control over Scotland's economic situation.

If not tied up to the Treasury on a daily basis, the Bank of England is moored to the same jetty, and on that jetty their joint thoughts are dictated by their personal location and responsibility for the south east and adjoining areas which are the main engines of the UK economy. The admission of needing to "level up" in the English north-eastern red wall constituencies is proof of past years of south east–centric policymaking.

There was not in the parliament elected in 2019, a single Treasury minister from a Scottish constituency. Of five MP Treasury ministers, four were located in the southern part of England, with only the Chancellor sitting for a Yorkshire one. There was not one Scot a member of the monetary policy committee. Indeed, its statutory members from within the Bank and the four external members were all anchored in the southern financial establishment. That make-up, excluding a Scottish input, has not changed with the 2024 election.

The dual influence of the Bank and the Treasury over the Scottish economy is inescapable. To them it would seem we must now add the Office for Budget Responsibility. Among the key levers on our economy not in Scottish government hands are currency, corporation tax, capital gains tax, dividend tax, inheritance tax, components of social security, investment incentives, business law, employment law, offshore oil and gas, fisheries, international trade relations, defence expenditure and immigration. That is the external control that does not allow the Holyrood parliament with its present set of devolved powers to create a genuine Scottish economy.

The model we have today – an external controlled economy – is the one that gives us GERS, with its consistent deficit, and the accompanying gibe about how lucky we are to be a subsidised part of the union.

It is to change that economic model that is the motivation for many who argue for independence. Not "Bring Back Control" because Scots have never had it, but "Take Control."

The argument deployed by unionists each time GERS is issued, is based on the fallacy that the economic model that gives us the much-trumpeted deficit, is the one that will continue in an independent Scotland. That is not what independence is being sought for.

It might seem trite, but what will what matter economically is how we use the sovereign powers of independence. As I write, the only official document we have as a guide so far to thinking on that level is the Scottish Government's National Strategy for Economic Transformation, published on the 1st of March 2022.

In terms of piety, the Strategy gets ten out of ten. There is "a new Net Zero Industrial Strategy" achieved by "our just transition" towards that aim, and "we will strive to build a nature-positive economy." The document is replete with words of green virtue.

There is no lack of words of intentions in the Strategy – "Our vision is to create a wellbeing economy: a society that is thriving across economic, social and environmental dimensions, and that delivers prosperity for all of Scotland's people and places. We aim to achieve this while respecting environmental limits, embodied in our climate and nature targets." It is difficult, amid a torrent of words that paint a picture of the Scotland we would all like to live in, to find hard concrete points of action that an SNP Government will take on independence to enable the entrepreneurs it so desires to emerge and business to flourish.

Another disturbing aspect of the SNP Government mindset, as revealed in the Strategy, is that it does not question the incompatibility of its aim of economic transformation from the present "relevant lack of business growth and persistent poverty" to one that will "establish Scotland as a world-class entrepreneurial nation founded on a culture that encourages, promotes and celebrates entrepreneurial activity in every sector of our economy" with its obsession with Net Zero. That obsession rules out the full use of Scotland's resources, and has negative implications on policies that are essential for Scotland's economic development.

Before explaining why this is so, let me say that while I depart from the Greens on their view that the increase in our planet's warming is an existential threat to human existence (for which we humans are to blame), there is validity in much of their concern about human effect upon our land, rivers, marine resources, the pollution of the oceans and seas with plastics and other materials, and the threat to continued existence of animal species and plants. It is a public good that people should engage in calling for policies in these fields to mitigate the consequences of human activity, even if sometimes the claims can be exaggerated (which is in the nature of special interest group activity) and sometimes wrongly conflated with climate issues.

For a different Scottish economy to emerge from the exercise of full sovereignty, we need a clear view of what Government is, and what it can and cannot do, and then assess what our needs are in economic policy.

The Role of Government Big or Small, Weak or Strong?

Just as we don't talk much about foreign affairs in Scotland, we rarely talk about governance. Gone are the days of John P. Mackintosh, Professor of Politics at Edinburgh University and Labour MP, writing standard works on the subject and commanding wide public attention to it.

The still unresolved ideological question that fundamentally separates Right from Left is about the role of Government as the instrument of the State. Small or large, minimal or extensive in its powers? Especially on matters that affect economic activity. Given the importance today not only of direct Government institutions like the NHS, but of the social security system, the term "economic activity" is a broad one. Wide ranging discussion leading to a conclusion on the role of the state is required from the movement well before any independence campaign takes place.

I tend to see that question as between "a weak state or strong state," rather than "big state or small state." A strong state need not stretch its tentacles nearly everywhere and in terms of human liberty, it should not do so. What matters is what a strong state can and must do on its own in the public interest, and how outside of the basic "musts" that it has responsibility for, it can contribute to economic development.

We live in a capitalist world where even the Marxist-Leninist Chinese Communist Party with its "socialism with Chinese characteristics" can blur that message but not hide it. Capitalism is a universal system but it operates at different levels of exploitation of resources and people in different parts of the world. For

Scotland, part of social-democratic Europe, it means in practice a mixed economy: that is, getting state and private sector in sensible balance. In that equation a strong-state, using its powers for policies aimed at the defence of labour, the promotion of an efficient public sector that serves the people, and a robust indigenous private sector, is essential. A strong indigenous private sector, rather than one over reliant on international capital, should be the aim of the movement's economic policy.

What is Government? What can and can't it do?

To govern means using state authority to maintain security, make laws, regulations, influence economic and social actors, provide essential public services, respond to internal and external events affecting the polity, and leading, swaying and gauging public opinion.

Government consists of transient ministers, SPADS, and a permanent civil service that executes ministerial policy via an administrative hierarchy – one that operates through layers of officials with authority to enact policies of the elected government. Ministers set the policy for a department, and the civil servants give effect to the policy by their actions on a day-to-day basis.

In Scotland now (and as it will be with independence), civil servants are recruited on the basis of educational, administrative or technical skills, and trained to professional levels. Ministers are drawn from the number MSPs who form a majority in the Parliament. There is no evidence of any party conducting formal or informal education or training of its members from whom it draws its candidates. In the Scottish Parliament, 65 MSPs would form a majority. Not all will be of ministerial calibre.

Ministers need to have an ability to monitor how their policies are being implemented, and this is done, if at all, through the very civil service that is tasked with the job of policy implementation. Ministerial "grip" on a department is vital, but not always there. The civil service is there to serve and protect ministers: it is not a risk-taking organisation and it is not one of the wealth creation sectors of society.

Over recent decades, in both the UK and at devolved level, governance has come from, not elected ministers, but unelected minister-appointed Quangos. Transport Scotland, which controls other Quangos such as CMAL and CalMac, is an example. Education Scotland is another. The NHS is run by twenty-two bodies including fourteen Health Boards. In total there are 132 Quangos, which is rather a lot for a country with a population of 5.4m. In theory, all are ultimately responsible to a Minister but in practice, these are self-directing instruments of a bureaucratic class rarely accountable to those ministers who appoint them. The most effective organisation for holding them accountable is the Auditor General, whose reports can lay bare just exactly how they are or aren't performing. It is difficult to find evidence that his strictures and revelations regarding their failure have led to a general improvement in the management of public affairs.

Government can create jobs directly through decisions related to the public sector, and indirectly in the private business sector through its macro-economic powers such as monetary policy, taxation, laws on company formation, employment rights, planning and regulation. It can seek to assist business development by creating arms-length agencies like Scottish Enterprise and the Scottish National Investment Bank, whose remit is set by ministers who also appoint its board members. It is perhaps time to consider whether these two should continue in an independent Scotland. The budget of the former has been cut, something that might raise the question of its continuing value. With regard to the National Investment Bank, it is a good example of the triumph of PR. It was launched giving the most emphasis to the £2bn investment figure, but that was a commitment over 10 years, making for only £200m a year, nothing like the investment level needed to take the opportunities available.

Take the potential of onshore and offshore wind. The SNIB reports that it has supported the offshore wind sector over the years by "investing just under £200 million across several projects, alongside approximately £700 million from third-party investors. These investments are aimed at addressing infrastructure bottlenecks, building a competitive supply chain in Scotland." Good work. But how much better would it be if we had a National Investment Bank with the capital to take equity, and therefore a share in the profits, of the whole Wind industry?

Where Government has a direct and crucial contribution to the economy is in Education, from nursery to university level, on energy supply, security, road, rail, ports, airports and broadband infrastructure. On government success or failure in those responsibilities sits the fate of the economy. It follows that the quality of the MSPs from which a government is formed matters.

Creating a different economy with independence We need to start with acquiring a different mentality

The acquisition of sovereignty will catapult Scotland's people to a higher level of self-responsibility domestically and internationally. This will be a new experience. The difference between independence and devolution is huge. Being a citizen of, and a government of, an independent state means you are in a "no excuse" zone. Your decisions carry consequences, for good or ill, and they are your decisions.

Take a look at the contrast between devolution and independence. Being a citizen of a devolved administration, and being an MSP in the devolved parliament with limited powers, leaves both free to find external scapegoats for errors – enabling citizen and MSPs (and devolved government ministers) to state opinions on a variety of matters without the cost that comes with giving effect to them. Virtue signalling is one of the perks that comes with devolution.

Independence means nowhere to hide. Every decision domestically is yours and yours alone. In foreign affairs you cannot denounce and lecture the Chinese Communist Party's governance of China without calculating the cost of its retaliation by closing it markets to key Scottish products or its withdrawal of students from universities. Your leaders cannot easily make a potential enemy by virtue signalling disapproval of a presidential candidate in the United States. The luxury of engaging in student politics is no longer available.

The changes independence requires each Scot to make

Whatever criticisms have been made about the Scottish Government's National Strategy, few would dissent from its identification of sectors where there is either excellent performance, such as in life sciences, or potential for development. But if we are going to change Scotland's economic performance and bring it to a higher and successful level when independent, then some honesty about the beams in our own eyes, and the principles we need to address, are required.

A sense of gladly grasping full responsibility, and willingness to escape from the present mindset with its in-built degree of dependency, will be essential. It will require a leap out of the present rut of provincialism that is the debilitating "gift" of devolution. It will require imagination – missing at present – and the need for public and private sectors to recognise they can be complementary rather than competitors for resources, with each having its different function in wealth creation. A hospital that takes in a sick or injured worker, and puts him/her back to work helps him/her go on to create wealth is an example of where an effective public service is an aid to the private sector. The same assistance to the private sector can be said for Scottish Water, public transport and, above all, Education.

What the people in Scotland are capable of, and what their ambitions are, is what is going to count. Having capability without the drive of ambition means deciding to live with limitations, not success.

There are some things in our outlook we need to change: cutting off the tallest thistle, the "him? I kent his faither" takedown, and our (selectively) inbuilt bias against elitism, which is a product of one of our social virtues, a broad egalitarianism – a legacy from the Reformation and Robert Burns. "Selectively" because we have a remarkable ability to compartmentalise our view on elitism. When Nicola Benedetti is recognised worldwide as an elite musician, we are delighted. When Sean Connery was among the elite of the elite of Hollywood, didn't we have a glow of satisfaction? When the elite footballer Henrik Larsen was banging in the goals for Celtic at the then incredible wage of £48,000 a week, all his Celtic fans were delighted. Andy Murray's elite status on the tennis circuit was a matter for national pride. Laura Muir, up there among the elite at the Olympics, was the nation's pride and joy. If only we had an elite squad to guarantee entry to all the World cups, how happy the Tartan Army would be!

If the five million plus Scots are to earn a good living in the years that lie ahead, we shall need the full powers of sovereignty and an unashamed ambition to be one of the elite small countries in the world. That will mean a change of mentality. I happen to believe that the dawn of full responsibility, with the Westminster scapegoat no longer available to excuse our own mistakes, will see us step up to the plate.

Principle factors to recognise and build upon

At present, as an integral part of the UK market with its population of 65m, Scotland's economic performance is heavily influenced by Keynesian demand management by the UK government. As the admission of the need to "level up" implies, this has enriched the southern part of the UK but failed to deliver to England's northern areas, and to Scotland. Keynesian policy prescription may impact as intended on what is the central part of the economy – England's south-east – but becomes diluted of effect when it reaches the outer regions.

There is every reason to expect that Keynesian demand management in an independent Scottish state will be no different. We will be a 5.4m population market with a central belt of around 3 million, and four other smaller and diverse areas: Grampian, Highlands and Islands, Borders, Dumfries and Galloway. Public spending stimulus by government to tackle problems in the largest part, the central belt, will not necessarily benefit to the same degree the other population areas.

So, there has to be a counterpart to demand management: resource management is the principle on which the new economic policy should rest. The twin aims of resource management should be to boost business and jobs which engage in the domestic market, and place greater emphasis than hitherto on those businesses exporting goods and services – the things that are internationally tradeable.

What matters in resource management is what indigenous assets a country has. Scotland is rich in these: People, Land, Energy, Water, Fisheries, Scenery, Heritage. But these are broad descriptions. What we need is something that has never been done in our small country – a complete audit of the Scottish economic base as it is now, identifying in detail what we have so that we know which parts (be it in the private or public sector) are excellent, good, passable or poor by the international standard along with the impact upon them of AI so that both government and the private sector, working together with real-time knowledge, can take measures to maintain excellence, boost good to excellent, and bring poor performance up to a better level: all for the purpose of creating a strong expansive indigenous economic base capable of creating wealth.

Take for example the small business sector that employs 1.2 million people. This can range from a one-person operation, to a café employing a few people, to a small local shop, to a company employing 250 in manufacturing. We need to know and understand it better so that government policies are designed to aid each sub-sector to develop and grow. One vital input missing in the SME sector is Research and Development. The sector simply cannot afford it. The kind of audit proposed will be able to identify where R&D can make a difference for SMEs, with a designated university, funded for this R&D purpose, feeding knowledge to the SMEs, and so assist in the growth of that sector.

It should be a defined responsibility of our universities to inform the people regarding the development and impact the AI revolution is having, and likely to have, on society and its economic base.

AI currently, and increasingly, will produce revolutionary changes in our economic base and the social structures built upon it. New ethical, political and economic issues will arise. Will AI, as is happening now, continue to concentrate power and wealth in relatively few hands? Can the idea of democracy, where the educated knowledgeable citizen has power over government, be reversed with government controlling the citizen? If robots displace humans in jobs and in the creation of wealth, where does that place those whose labour is no longer required? AI can create wealth, but how will it be distributed?

To grapple with and resolve these questions, and many

others, with the aim of maintaining a power-balanced society will require citizens with knowledge of the economic and social forces shaping the world they live in. Public education beyond the format that exists today will be needed. That should be an extension of the educational responsibilities that fall to universities and colleges.

In recent years, during which new technologies have developed, those who own them have taken a greater share of the wealth created than labour. A knowledgeable, critically-minded citizenry will be vital for the continuation of democracy, and that in turn will need policies to ensure that the potential for inequality that is part of the AI revolution does not become inequality baked into the system.

There is no alternative to a mixed economy, in which market forces play a significant role. The Socialist varieties of central demand management have been tried and failed. A mixed economy policy is not a surrender of the Left to capitalism but a balance between the power of capital and the countervailing power of the collective. An economy subject only to full market forces would mean labour's surrender to capital, and inevitable gross inequality that cannot but produce social division. Trial and error since 1945 in Western Europe produced the mixed economy as the alternative to unfettered capital.

It is the division of power in a mixed economy that creates the need for a strong state. We can acknowledge the role of the private sector as the main engine of wealth creation but clear boundaries must be set around its power and influence and how it operates in a democratic society has to be made compatible with the public interest. Exercising judgement to accomplish that balance is the role of the state.

Scotland's human capital
The role of Education

People are the basic resource that an economy is built upon. Disraeli's dictum that "*Upon the education of the people of this country the fate of this country depends*" applies in spades to a small country that has to find its living in a global economy. Singapore proved that truth. With only its harbour as another natural resource when becoming independent in 1965, its government placed emphasis on the excellence of its education and human development as the foundation of its success. Singapore's GDP per capita is $84,734, Scotland's is $50,002 including oil and gas, from which we get little direct benefit so that figure is too high to be accurate.

We are not Singapore with the culture that enabled Lee Kwan Yew to dictate and drive through policies. Although we are gifted with many more natural resources than he had at his disposal, we can take a lesson from him on the role of education, where he succeeded in producing an elite population with a stunningly successful economy.

For an independent Scotland to succeed in education, we need to admit that we have children born to fail, because we have not come to grips with the link of poverty at home with a school's ability to inspire pupils and students to high achievement.

Our young now, and in the immediate future, enter education in a world that will pose unprecedented problems and challenges as the technological revolution develops in ways that cannot be forecast, in a world that is changing rapidly now that all nations, no longer just some nations, are seeking prosperity.

Our young people have to be equipped for this new world. Thinking critically. Applying intellectual rigour. These are two indispensable tools of the human mind that are fundamental to their ability to cope with what is to come for citizens of a democracy who must co-exist with others that do not share that value. A population that questions, probes, analyses, and is sceptical until convinced, is a well prepared one.

Here, based on my own experience, I have a suggestion to make: teach an outline of philosophy at S2, and take students into deeper areas in S3 and S4.

My experience was that I left school without what was then the Scottish School Leaving Certificate. I was not dumb. I had qualified for entry to the selective Ayr Academy and made nothing of the opportunity it offered. Partly my fault and partly that of the school. I joined the Royal Navy as a radio operator and spent two and a half years with the Army in a small combined operations unit in Hong Kong. I had always been political, and in that unit met a regular soldier, Tony O'Donnell and others whom while doing their national service, took political discussion and debate as normal. We were lucky with our Commanding Officer who organised a discussion session once a week on current events.

I had always read books and continued to do so. The Young Women's Association in Kowloon had a library to which we had access. I picked up Bertrand Russell's *The Problems of Philosophy*. It was at first hard going for my untutored mind but it changed me forever. It taught me to question before accepting what seemed the obvious and often was not, to be sceptical of the views and policies punted by those in authority, and to apply intellectual rigour to ideas and policies that are proposed by those claiming to know best, along with my own ideas.

I was, as a young MP, paid a private compliment by a journalist when he said I had an ability to drill down into a subject and get at its roots. That ability was the benefit that book bestowed on me.

In an age where the young, who are tomorrow's policymaking or policy supporting adults, are swamped with information and misinformation, they should at school be armed with the set of critical tools that philosophy offers.

Chapter 6
A small nation needs the best educated people

Schools

Given the OECD results the Curriculum can't be that Excellent

Long gone are the days when Scottish education was regarded worldwide as one of the best. The reason for that deserved reputation was what education historians described as a "firm foundation in disciplinary knowledge." As Professor Lindsay Paterson (whom I quote below from a Talk he gave to the Royal Philosophical Society of Glasgow on 5th March 2025) has noted "that is not how the Scottish School curriculum has been in recent years," with the result being a very different, poorer, reputation than it had previously.

"The evidence for the changes that have caused decline are set out in the OECD three-yearly Programme for International Student Assessment" testing fifteen-year-olds.

"In reading, Scottish attainment has been flat since 2006 (after a steep fall from the beginning of the century). In Mathematics, Scotland declined steadily from 2006 to 2018, and then fell sharply to 2022, after Covid. In science, there has been a steady decline in

Scotland since 2006, gentle at first and then steep, and with no evidence that Covid affected the rate of decline." England, he records, judged on the same test, "has been going in the opposite direction." He puts this difference down to the English curriculum being "increasingly focused on knowledge" which is not the case in Scotland where "skills" are emphasised. He points out that England is "not alone in halting decline by redefining its school curriculum on the basis of knowledge: there are similar experiences in Poland, Germany, Japan and Massachusetts."

It isn't that our children are without education, it is that as things stand now the standard of rigour is missing, of the kind that would endow them with a better education. And in a world in which other nations have caught up and are passing us, a better education than is given now is imperative if they are to succeed.

This flaw in the system now compared with the 1980s is illustrated by these two examples, among others, advanced by Professor Paterson. They apply to the 5-14 age groups: (a) today's curriculum requirement of a pupil is "Through developing my knowledge of context clues, punctuation, grammar and layout, I can read unfamiliar texts with increasing fluency, understanding and expression' (b) in the 1980s, pupils were expected to 'know, understand and... use at least the following terms: vowel and consonant; adjective, adverb, pronoun and conjunction; masculine and feminine; singular and plural; tense; paragraph."

Note the difference. One (a) is broad brush, whereas (b) is specific about what is expected to be learnt.

Higher Education: Universities and Colleges
Universities

Universities are central to the worth of a society. From them flows the benefits to all of expanding the universe of knowledge along with the exploration of and advancement of science. If an independent ambitious Scotland is to join the group of elite nations, we shall need our universities to reach and sustain a standard of academic excellence and for a core curriculum to be genuinely world class. In the *Sunday Times* Guide of 131 UK universities, five Scottish ones are in the top twenty, one is ranked 44, two others are in the top fifty, one ranked 59, one ranked 61, one at 63, and the other two 105 and 121. The University of the Highlands and Islands is not covered in the survey. Those rankings are not good enough. We spend £2bn a year on Universities and Colleges. Is that spread too thinly over too many?

Alex Salmond is no longer with us, the seas have not gang dry, but an inescapable truth is that the funding model for universities that was the inevitable outcome of his policy – high fees from lots of foreign students and low fees from the Scottish government for Scottish domiciled ones – is not working, and is the cause of the financial crisis with cuts of courses accompanied by people being sacked.

My instinct is in favour of free university and college tuition for Scots. That is born of the belief that there should be no financial barrier to anyone advancing to the highest levels of personal education, along with some discomfort that charging students fees through state loans saddles a young person earning a degree with a load of debt as is the case in England.

There is nothing basically wrong with the model. Foreign students in our universities, especially those who are post-graduate, bring intellectual, cultural and social perspectives often different from our own and thus help us better understand the world we live in. Taking the future into account, a diverse foreign student body gives Scotland links to the future leaders of countries we will do business with, and engage with in the geopolitical world. That government should fund Scottish students is a given, not simply on moral grounds, but because it is essential for the economic life of the nation to have a well- educated population.

I doubt if in our remaining devolution years any government at Holyrood will have the will to tackle the university funding problem. Those who take over on independence will not be able to dodge it. It must be one of the priorities for the first independent government. There are two bullets that need bitten. Do we have too many universities and are mergers the answer? And, if there is a belief in free tuition, will it be fully funded with no cap on Scottish student numbers?

Colleges

I think I am correct in writing that Colleges get much less public attention than universities, and consequently in policymaking, yet in terms of enhancing the education and life chances of students alongside the contribution their students make to the economic position of the nation, they are equal in value to the universities.

The range of courses they provide of direct relevance to the needs of the economy is impressive, and they also offer a way into university education for mature students and late developers. As I write, Colleges too are facing a financial crisis and again I doubt if their problems will be adequately addressed by the devolution parliament, as it is the very organisation that has allowed the crisis to grow. Necessity will drive the independent Parliament to do so if it gets its first priorities right – one of which will be to house the thousands who have no permanent home.

To provide affordable homes to rent or buy in sufficient number, Scotland will need to build no fewer than 50,000 a year, year on year, and that will require a building workforce that we do not have at present. Construction businesses and Colleges working together will be needed to create the workforce that, even with AI interventions, will be needed.

Adequate funding for staff costs and a better grants-bursary system for students will make a priority call on central government cash, but more is needed to elevate the importance of the Colleges in the public's assessment of their role in education, and to give college education a higher level of prestige compared to universities than at present.

Earlier, I have suggested merging universities. That would entail making a number of lecturers redundant which would be a waste of talent. Some courses and the lecturers who deliver them could be incorporated within the Colleges, offering students first-year level university standard introduction to history, literature, philosophy, and sciences, thus enhancing College academic standing in the eyes of the public and students.

The Jim McColl Junior College experiment
Time to re-enact

To his credit, Jim McColl conceived and partly funded the Newlands Junior College in Glasgow, aimed at those young people aged 14-16 who were not academic and were heading nowhere. He paid in **£5m**. The Scottish Government contributed half a million pounds as a capital grant and thereafter contributed substantially to its running costs, as did Glasgow City Council. It was funded for five years.

McColl and the experienced staff recruited saw this as a demonstration model of what an educational institution, designed for a group who were "disengaged" from school, could do to prevent them from drifting to nowhere and a life without accomplishment.

The hope was that once this Junior College proved a success in providing structured educational support and encouragement to a cohort not given priority within the educational system, it would be replicated across Glasgow and other parts of the country.

The Newlands Junior College was successful. For the students it gave them status and with that came self-confidence and a readiness to engage in the educational opportunities now on offer. A key part of the intention was to link the College to local businesses and it had an outstanding record in getting its graduates into jobs.

Although I had no public position, I asked if I could visit and was welcomed. The young people I met were akin to me and four of my classmates at Ayr Academy, where we too were disengaged from School. Just like us when we left school, they had none or few qualifications. Just like us, the schools they attended didn't stimulate their interests, and just like us, they were seen as members of a cohort that would drift around not likely to make much of a career in anything.

But enrolling in a college gave them status and being treated as young adults by experienced staff got the message across that they mattered. With the College's links with the business community, and what they were learning, they had the idea they were going somewhere – into jobs offering skills and opportunity.

There was a high cost for each student. Jim McColl estimates the cost for each Junior College student as £15,000 per year, compared to £7,000 for a secondary school pupil. Glasgow City Council was unable to take on that financial cost, and so after five years, Newlands closed.

On the face of it, fair enough. Yes, the model worked but the cost was, in the eyes of Councillors and Scottish Government, too high. But if we place the Junior College in the context of the Scottish Government's declared aim to "close the attainment gap", we can reach a different conclusion. The cohort the Junior College was designed for were never going to be part of the "gap" to be narrowed in the primary-secondary system. They were never in the attainment equation.

The reason for narrowing the attainment gap in regular schools is to give every young person the chance of a good start in adult life, thus narrowing the employment and wage gap in adult life. In that context of narrowing attainment and expanding what could happen in adult life, the student cost of Junior College is a worthwhile investment.

I made reference earlier to me and my three classmates whom the Rector of Ayr Academy told us would make nothing of ourselves. There was a logic to his reasoning.

We were failures. Disengaged from school. The four of us did make something of ourselves because we had something within us that school had failed to bring out. With a 95% success rate in placing its students in jobs, Newlands brought out ability and talent in its young people that otherwise many of them would never know they had.

My hope is that an independent Scottish Government, when it comes to a comprehensive review of education, will recognise that Junior Colleges can be as important as any other section, and will be prepared to fund them.

What about the children born to fail?

It was in 1973 that "Born to Fail" entered the educational lexicon in a book produced by the National Children's Bureau. It was based on an extensive study of all children in England, Scotland and Wales born in the week 3-9 March 1958, with information on them gathered at the age of seven, and again aged eleven.

The study showed "that the adversities of some boys and girls can extend into almost every aspect of their health, their family circumstances, and their educational development; it shows the enormous inequalities of life for the 'disadvantaged' compared with 'ordinary' children. It questions some of the priorities, perspectives and seeming indifference of British society itself."

Nothing has changed for many children. Children born to fail do not live in families with good or steady income, with secure housing. They are born in what we call "deprived areas" where income levels are low, where many exist on benefits, where single mothers struggle to survive, where some families have never had anyone in work, and where poverty damages personalities and saps energy.

Those who have never been poor cannot ever understand, even when most sympathetic, what it is like to engaged in a daily struggle to survive and what that struggle can do to the human personality, and how it can fracture families. That's being poor. Trapped poverty is worse. We have to our national shame 25% of Scottish children in poverty, with 80,000 in abject poverty. How else can they be other than born to fail?

To their credit, the Blair-Brown government sought to address the problem with their Sure Start programme bringing resources and trained personnel to hubs designed to tackle the multiple problems inherent in the deprived areas. "Where is the programme now?" is the question in a recently written paper showing it has been consistently cut back since Brown left office.

Full time nursery and health care – an essential step

Narrowing the educational attainment gap in primary and secondary schools can only be accomplished by addressing the pre-primary circumstances afflicting children in the 1-5 age groups in the areas of acute social deprivation. This in turn can only done by the provision, and requirement of compulsory attendance at, a combination of nursery and health care Children's Centres in each area, full-time Monday to Friday.

You may be surprised at "compulsory attendance." I am not a softie socialist. One of the by-products of poverty is often the lack of responsibility, arising out of the lack of structures requiring sustained self-discipline. It is just as logical to require compulsory attendance at a nursery school for disadvantaged children, as it is to make attendance at primary and secondary school compulsory for all children. It is time to make all children be born with a chance of success. Families mired in poverty cannot do that. The state can.

Pie in the sky?

I would not be surprised if anyone who has read so far has come to the conclusion that my call for resource allocations (mainly money) to the full range of educational support, along with the need for a housing programme and the reconstruction of the NHS, is a "pie in the sky" wish list from an old socialist.

If so, you would be wrong. I was brought up by Ayrshire socialists who, like Nye Bevan, believed the language of socialism lay in the ability to define what were priorities for spending "the people's money" to meet the people's needs.

If Scotland is to be lifted out of the rut it is in today, and aims to be a successful small elite nation, it will need to start with the priorities, the essentials of what the public services need to contribute, and that will require addressing the structure of governance so that it is slimmed down to ensure the necessary resources flow in the right direction, with effect.

Without an education system that embraces all our children with the gift of opportunity the Scottish nation will not succeed and poverty will not be abolished. Without an adequate affordable housing supply families will struggle economically, educationally and socially, and so will the nation as a whole. If the NHS is not reconstructed and managed better, it will continue to drain cash needed elsewhere. That is not "pie in the sky". It is the reality facing this nation today, and will be the reality facing the first independent government.

People I have listened to have doubts about whether any government can deliver on what is needed. There is a lack of confidence in the political system, and a view beginning to emerge that delivery of the right policies is hard to do.

They are not hard to do. That is, if you have a government with the courage to tell the truth, spell out the choices, get the priorities right, concentrate on them, and not be diverted by the political winds that blow as single-issue pressure groups clamour to attend to them before all else.

Thirty-two education authorities for a small nation?

The present structures are wasteful of money that could be better allocated to schools. Scotland has thirty-two local councils all responsible for providing primary and secondary education. Some have Directors of Education, some Head of Schools, some where the official responsible for education has other responsibilities. Until recently in one authority, South Ayrshire, the Chief Executive had education as just one of his responsibilities. Thirty-two local councils, and so thirty-two sets of administrations, soaking up the education budgets. That system has been in place since the Westminster Parliament passed The Scottish Local Government Act 1993. "Sell-by date" comes to mind, especially when the facts show that the system is failing to deliver to all of our children.

If we are to provide an education to all of our children at the level which will enable them, as mature citizens of Scotland, to be equal in proven ability to anyone else from any other nation, and capable of responding successfully to the demands imposed by the challenges of swiftly evolving sciences and technologies, then the present educational structure will have to go and be replaced.

Replaced, I suggest, by a much smaller number of Joint Boards of Education, where local councils combine for this one specific responsibility, funded directly by a Ministry of Education headed by a Cabinet Minister. An example is Ayrshire, where at present there are three councils responsible for education where one used to do better. Another is Lanarkshire which has two authorities, while in the east we have Edinburgh, East Lothian, Midlothian and West Lothian. A further reform should be in the role of Head Teacher, where he/she should have the ability to hire and fire all staff, and thus gain the necessary autonomy, and full responsibility, for a school's performance. Restructuring local government education, with more power for heads at school level, with just one source of funding (the Ministry) would see a better allocation of resources between the administration and the schools where our children go.

The creation of joint boards should also produce a benefit that gets little attention these days: the importance of the Director of Education. The person in this role should be an outstanding educationalist, acting as the leader and guide of the teaching staff in the local education system, setting standards, spotting and promoting future head teachers, and with detailed knowledge of each school. A Director of Education of stature would be one of the most important voices listened to in the development of educational philosophy at national level.

With thirty-two education authorities, each providing a mall patch rather than a large platform of the kind that would attract big thinkers and doers, there is little prospect of the kind of Directors of Education we need. A reconstruction from thirty-two to seven or eight education authorities should assist in putting that right.

Land and its use

Land and who owns it, is an issue of long standing in Scotland, but one that comes and goes in our politics. Legislative and executive action has been taken from time to time to transfer ownership of some island and other acreages to communities. But there is no national land policy that can ensure it corresponds to its most sensible use between completing claims, and measures the actions of landowners (a number of whom are absentee) with what is in the national interest.

Brian Wilson (The Herald, 7th of June 2022) put it better than I can: "I always find it curious that so many who talk endlessly about Scotland as their guided entity are so little concerned with the fact that a high proportion of it is run as private kingdoms, largely immune to public policy unless there is money to be made. Land for housing? Certainly not. Maintenance of population? Not our problem. Public access? Not if we can help it." In mentioning private kingdoms, he might have had in mind, as an example, the West Highland estates owned by the ruler of Dubai.

The occupation of land by owners and what they use it for, or what they don't use it for, is a matter of national interest. Forests are planted to enable people from outside Scotland to avoid tax or by hedge funds in order to gain carbon credits on which they can make a profit. In one case, a young family who sought land to create a food productive farm were outbid by a hedge fund intent on tree planting for tax purposes.

In certain rural areas landownership is power – power that can prevent social housing development, power to determine its use for a narrow interest, power to set labour conditions and wages, power to decide that land is purely for private recreational use. That such power lies in the hands of some people who have no commitment to the economic life of a community or the nation, and whose domicile is not Scotland, is a nonsense. Land made productive, with both domestic consumption and international trade at its heart, has to be part of the broad strategic plan to create a new economy.

Land is at present a taxable base that is not taxed. Were a land value tax imposed, one estimate is that it would bring in around £1.5bn a year. This can be done under devolution powers, but is not likely to happen. It will be another necessary action under independence if our first sovereign government is to reconstruct the economy.

*

Farmers are one of the most essential group of workers in every country, as it is by their efforts that food is produced. In Scotland, their access to land, either through owner-occupancy or tenancies, is fundamental to our food security which is a strategic national interest.

I am not suggesting the nationalisation of land, but advocating for an active national policy that has at its core two principles: one, that absentee landowners should be required to sell their land in the Highlands and Islands to Highland and Island Enterprise, who would then make it available on long lease to tenant farmers, or sell to new owner farmers, while those landowners elsewhere would be required to set aside substantial areas of land to long leased tenant farmers, or to outright purchase for farming purposes.

Chapter 7
Outside of Venezuela, Scotland is the only nation to discover oil, see it produced, and watch large numbers of its people get poorer. What an achievement!

For some time now, we in Scotland have been encouraged to discount any potential benefit from the oil and gas in the North Sea and the Clair field west of Shetland. Indeed, we have been told it is not an asset but a threat to the human race caused by rising earth temperatures, for which fossil fuels use and their emissions of vast quantities of CO_2 are responsible.

Any independent Scottish parliament and government which is serious about investing in the reconstruction of the economy will need capital, and the source of substantial capital is the oil and gas that lies under the waters within our jurisdiction. This chapter sets out why the present policy on oil and gas is wrong, so that what is now regarded as a liability to humanity, is seen as a vital plus that would be sheer stupidity to ignore.

We have been told that CO_2 is a pollutant, a proposition endorsed by a ruling of the United States Supreme Court in April 2007: that the world is heating up to dangerous levels because human activity in the use of fossil fuels is *producing more and more* CO_2, *that large areas of the Arctic and Antarctic will melt and seas will rise and swamp cities and small islands (with the latter first to experience this calamity), and this is all true because the IPCC says it is. The accepted narrative is that the IPCC is backed by 97 per cent of the science community, that it is an indisputable truth that humanity faces a* CO_2*-created existential threat of an apocalypse, and anyone who does not believe all that is a "climate change denier."*

Broadcasters like the BBC concluded some years ago that the science was "settled" with no need for its viewers and listeners to hear any alternative case. That message has been successful in convincing a majority that we are in a climate crisis and that CO_2 is the culprit.

The US Supreme Court was wrong. CO_2 is one of the building blocks of life. If by some miracle we were to eliminate it, or reduce it to a very low level, there would be no food and we would all die of starvation. Tomato growers, seeking to encourage plant growth, do not pollute their greenhouses when deliberately increasing the levels of CO_2 within them.

At a meeting of political activists, I asked the audience how much CO_2 was in the atmosphere. The answer was "lots." That has been roughly the answer I have received when asking that question of other people. One third-year university student said that CO_2 was like a blanket round the earth.

Fact: The total weight of the earth's atmosphere is 5.5 quadrillion metric tons – that is 5,500,000,000,000 metric tons. The table below gives atmospheric gases per cent volume, parts per million, and their mass in gigatons. Note the miniscule quantity of anthropogenic carbon dioxide.

GASES	Percentage volume	Parts per million	Mass in Gigatons
Nitrogen	77.8	780,840	3,897.821
Oxygen	20.9	209,500	1,194.327
Argon	0.9	9,340	66,581
Water vapour	0.4	4,000	12,024
Carbon dioxide (total including anthropogenic carbon dioxide)	0.04	429	3,252
Anthropogenic carbon dioxide	0.002	20.9	163

Reference: Koutsoyiannis, D. https://www.itia.ntua.gr/en/docinfo/2474/
Full text: p34 equation 67

I have often asked people who told me the world was heading for a heating hell what is the largest greenhouse gas in the atmosphere? None of them, although convinced of the climate emergency, have ever known the answer. It is water vapour.

*

The Maldives is a series of low-lying islands in the Indian Ocean. On the 17th of October 2009, its

Ministers donned Scuba gear and held the world's first ever underwater Cabinet meeting to emphasise how vulnerable their islands were to the rising waters that were going to be the catastrophic consequences of climate change.

This stunt would not have taken place if they had read the book written at that time by Swedish Professor Nils-Axel Morner (1938-2020) who was part of a team of researchers from the International Union for Quaternary Research examining the claim of the Maldives' government regarding the threat of rising sea levels . (Quaternary provides scientists with enormously rich records of past environmental and climate changes at time scales ranging from sub-annual to several million years).

In his book which sets out the team's scientific evidence, the conclusion is unambiguous: "We find no traces what so ever of any on-going sea level rise – it is all a myth – and we are hence able to free the Maldives from the condemnation to become flooded."

Not only did the Professor make the book available at nominal cost so that the Maldives government could purchase many copies for lots of people to read and understand, he wrote to its prime minister several times asking if he wanted to meet, so that he could emphasise by personal explanation that the country was under no threat from rising seas. The prime minister never took up the offer.

That didn't surprise him. In the book on the wider issue of the IPCC and the climate emergency, he noted: what the IPCC "scenarios predicted were the ultimate truth. Field observations indicating the opposite were dismissed as not reliable. Many scientific magazines closed their space for non-glorifying papers. Whilst enormous amounts of money were spent on IPCC-positive research, less and less (if any) were admitted to persons and projects of different opinion."

Ten years later, on 13th June 2019, the UN Secretary General, fully clothed, stood up to his thighs in the water off the coast of the tiny Pacific islands of Tuvalu. The press was well briefed, and the desired article the stunt produced asserted that "rising seas threaten to submerge" the island and "wipe" its ten thousand inhabitants "off the map entirely."

This is now 2025. The Maldives has lengthened its international airport runway to take the biggest aircraft to bring in more tourists. It has engaged in extensive infrastructure linking islands and intensified its tourist developments. Maldives adverts on CNN and other media platforms shows its most enticing properties lie right at water level. As the Cabinet now meets on land one must presume, given the investment, that it deems the Maldives safe from the rising sea.

The UN Secretary-General ruined a good suit based on the wrong information. Far from Tuvalu disappearing, the land has increased by 2.9 percent. Sea levels have risen and erosion does take place but is counteracted for by the rising sea breaking up old coral and landing it as sand thus creating the net gain of land. A study for *Nature* concluded that these dynamics mean that the islands of Tuvalu will "persist as sites for habitation over the next century." Those same dynamics are at work elsewhere, in Kiribati and the Marshall Islands.

The UN Secretary-General Antonio Guterres is a leading advocate of the climate change nightmare. Which brings me to the claim of 97 per cent of scientists having settled on a "scientific consensus." That figure was not the result of a worldwide poll of all scientists with knowledge of climate. It was the conclusion of a study of 928 scientific papers containing references to global climate change, by Professor Naomi Oreskes – a historian of science.

In the real world of science, a large body of eminent scientists have been at pains to explain that "consensus is not science, and science isn't consensus." The day after the Secretary-General proclaimed a climate emergency, 500 earth and atmospheric scientists, engineers and professionals with knowledge of climate issues, wrote to him explaining there was no such emergency. They made several points. Natural as well as anthropogenic factors cause warming. Warming is far slower than predicted. Climate policy relies on inadequate models. CO_2 is a plant food essential to life. More CO_2 is beneficial for nature, greening the earth and increasing yields in crops worldwide. Climate policy must respect scientific and economic realities.

But like the Maldives government, the Secretary-General did not want to hear opinions which did not fit with the climate crisis consensus. Nothing has changed; the consensus is now a religion where faith excludes any counter view, however real. Take the BBC Radio 4 programme *Rethink*, which repeated claims of the consensus that crop yields could fall by 30 per cent by 2050 as a result of climate change. That forecast skipped over the reality of crop yield increases in the period of 2011-20: Maize up by 11.9%, potatoes 10.3%, Soy Beans 10.3%, Wheat 9.8%, and Rice 3.5%.

Professor Morner and those 500 were not a fringe group. Many scientists have weighed in against the consensus claims but such are the vested interests in maintaining that position, with reputations and large research grants at stake, that they are excluded from the mainstream outlets from where the general public get their information.

A classic case of counter opinion being ignored by governments and mainstream media was the publication of *Challenging "Net Zero" with Science* by Richard Lindzen, Alfred P. Sloan Professor (Emeritus of Atmospheric Science Foundation Massachusetts Institute of Technology), and William Happer (Professor of Physics Emeritus at Princeton University.) They published under the auspices of the CO_2 Coalition, which has a very large membership of scientists, engineers and others with relevant specialities.

Their detailed document effectively, scientifically demolishes the consensus that demonises fossil fuels and CO_2. It is available on the Web for those who want to be informed.

In their Executive Summary these are some of the points they make:

- Net Zero proponents regularly report that extreme weather is more severe and frequent because of climate change while the evidence shows no increase – and in some cases, a decrease – in such events.
- Computer models supporting every government Net Zero regulation and the trillions of dollars subsidizing renewables and electric cars, trucks, home heating, appliances do not work.
- Scientific research and studies that do not support the "consensus" narrative of harmful man-made global warming are routinely censored and excluded from government reports such as the IPCC.
- *Conclusions of the IPCC that contradict the narrative of catastrophic global warming from fossil fuels are*

rewritten by government bureaucrats for public reports to support the false narrative of Net Zero. (emphasis added)

- The many benefits of modest warming and increasing carbon dioxide are routinely either eliminated or minimised in government reports.
- The adoption of Net Zero is the rejection of overwhelming scientific evidence that there is no risk of catastrophic global warming caused by fossil fuels and CO_2.

The reader will know that those opposed to the "consensus" are labelled "climate change deniers" – a reaction similar to what comes from a religious body that, to protect its belief, must damn anything that threatens its doctrine as heresy. I have never once read or heard any scientist or lay person denying that earth's climate changes and that the world has warmed to 1.1C above the temperature of 1850 – except perhaps Donald Trump. With him however it is difficult, given his limited vocabulary and his style of one-liners, to know what it was he actually denounced as a "hoax."

The earth has warmed 1.1C since the end of the little ice age, coincident with the onset of the industrial revolution around 1850. In my life, from delivering milk as a boy in the late 1940s, when winters were long, bitter cold and snowfall and ice normal to playing golf in January 2025 as an 87-year-old, I have experienced climate change.

Many, many generations before me experienced great changes in the climate. Today's Saharah desert was once a plush region with an abundance of water, plants and animals. Between 200 BC and the sixth century AD, our ancestors experienced the Roman Warming, with higher temperatures than we experience today. In Tudor times temperatures dropped significantly, and in England from September 1955 to March 1556 unrelieved torrential rain brought great floods, drowning both people and cattle. Periods of warming followed, but the downward trend persisted and our recent ancestors had to tackle life in the little ice age, during which the Thames froze, seas froze around the coasts of Europe, and Glaciers advanced dramatically. Natural forces, not actions by humans, were what was at work.

The great natural forces in our world are by no means perfectly captured by models. The Club of Rome's book *The Limits to Growth*, published in 1972, based on a global computer model designed at MIT, made limits to growth, like climate change now, *the* issue of its times. It sold 3m copies immediately but has been proved wrong with both developed and developing countries growing and growing, with growth in the latter taking millions out of abject poverty.

We should be wary of computer model predictions. Modelling doesn't have a good record. When the "mad cow disease" (CJD) appeared in 1986 the model forecasts put heads in a spin. On Newsnight, 500,00 deaths were declared by a scientist as "not impossible." The Observer went into overdrive telling us, based on scientific modelling, that the death rate would be 500,000 deaths each year, with a network of National Euthanasia Clinics "struggling to help 500 people a week to a dignified death before brain disease robs them of reason and self-control." Nothing like it happened.

We should also be wary, indeed sceptical, of alarmist chants of "climate blame" pointing to human activity each time there is a large forest fire, a hurricane, heavy rain, or a drought. In 1900 the US port of Galveston was hit by a Force 4 hurricane that killed 8,000 people. The 2024 forest fires in California, for example, were due to rank bad forest management, as later acknowledged, and a poorly maintained electricity supply system. The physical damage to buildings we witness now as hurricanes hit mainland USA is more extensive than previously, but that is due to the increase in population of that country from 149m in 1945 to 330m today. A bigger population has built more that can be damaged.

*

Climate change is a natural phenomenon. Great natural forces are at work well outside the control of humanity – one such being the great ocean currents that act like conveyor belts distributing heat around the world.

The most important natural force of all is the sun. Without its activity and heat generated, there would be no life on earth and the scientific community lacks knowledge about the sun. Don't take my word for it. Take NASA's. It was only in 2018 that the first ever attempt to get scientific instruments near to the Sun was launched by NASA's Parker Solar Probe. It got to 3.8m miles above the sun's surface on 24th December 2024, giving scientists, in NASA's words the "potential to change our understanding of the Sun's mysterious processes" and bring us "closer than ever to unlocking the sun's deepest and most enduring mysteries."

Science has extensive knowledge of this planet and of external forces. But that knowledge is limited. As science, and we, celebrate as it pushes out the frontiers of knowledge, it, and we, should recognise science is also always standing on the brink of ignorance. The more complex the matter studied, and that certainly applies to the Sun, the planet and its climate, claims of science certainty should always be questioned.

Scientists don't know everything about what affects and makes our climate as NASA's admission of the Sun's mysteries shows. Given those mysteries yet to be understood about the Sun, and the other natural forces at work, the idea that we humans, by control of CO_2 emissions, can calibrate earth's temperature so as not to exceed by 1.5C that measured in 1850, is a claim beyond our ability to prove.

The IPCC

I suspect that for most who read that highlighted comment above from Professors Lindzen and Happer, about bureaucratic intervention to create false reports by the IPCC, will come as a surprise, such is the reputation governments and NGOs have given to that organisation. What those NGOs, the Greens and governments tell us is that the IPPC delivers a climate gospel that is the truth, the whole truth and nothing but the scientific truth. Not quite.

CLINTEL – the Climate Intelligence Foundation published a book in 2023 – *The Frozen Climate Views of the IPCC* – that analysed the IPCC Sixth Assessment (AR6). The authors findings on substance did not differ from others' critical assessments whom I have noted previously, so there will be no repetitious quoting. What is relevant to quote here is how it debunks the belief of the IPCC as the single guiding light on policy, whose reports are concrete evidence of the science consensus.

The book noted: "The Assessment cycle spanned 8 years and yielded 7 volumes. The IPCC is no longer a single entity, instead it now consists of numerous "Big Panels" which have less and less in common with one another. Each one produces large reports, sometimes thousands of pages, with contributions from hundreds of scientists and social scientists from all around the world. In this cycle for example the WG1 report was 2409 pages long, and the WG2 report was even longer with 3068 pages and the WG3 reported also contained 2913 pages.

Apart from the sprawling nature of the reports, the IPCC is also a "Big Player" in the sense that it dominated the narrative on climate change, although the nature of its influence is deceptive. People speak as if there is a single 'view' attributable to the IPCC which is the 'consensus' of the thousands of participating expert authors and reviewers. This picture of the IPCC makes it hard to criticize those who claim to be invoking the consensus position. Yet it is doubtful that any of the IPCC contributors or reviewers ever read all seven volumes, nor were any asked to indicate their agreement with everything therein. Since, on many important topics, the chapters describe conflicting lines of evidence and admit to only limited levels of agreement or confidence, it is not plausible to suppose that the IPCC holds a single view on every given topic.

Yet the media routinely invokes the IPCC as a unified body putting forward a simple clear (and dire) message, and politicians rely on this message to justify their climate policies. The IPCC has become a 'knowledge monopolist' and this brings all kinds of dangers into play."

The IPCC is a flawed system, but its name and "climate change" is parroted by those in authority positions in defence of Net Zero policies. These are proving to be an exercise in economic self-harm and exceptionally damaging to the lives of young people who have been led to believe the world is heading for an early hell-fire end.

To their credit, as I have noted earlier, there are scientists and others with the necessary expertise who have sought and continue to seek to refute the basis on which the consensus has rested. There is the *Nongovernmental International Panel on Climate Change* (NIPCC) established by scientists and scholars which is "wholly independent of political pressures and influences and therefore is not predisposed to produce politically motivated conclusions or policy recommendations."

It describes the IPCC as "*government sponsored, politically motivated, and predisposed to believing that climate change is a problem in need of a U.N. solution." NIPCC was set up after scientists assessed the IPCC 4th Assessment Report in 2003, and came to the view that the "IPCC was biased with respect to making future projections of climate change, discerning a significant human-induced influence on current and past climatic trends, and evaluating the impact of potential carbon dioxide-induced environmental changes in the Earth's biosphere.*"

Are the Scots a sane nation or the saftest in the world family?

I have devoted a good part of this chapter to the climate change issue, hoping that the information I have conveyed, which is not widely known, will enable change in policy towards the use of our oil and gas energy resources.

Any sane nation, and any sane political party, in a country that needs investment like its people need oxygen, would be trying to work out how to get Scottish Governmental hands on at least some of the oil production and cease being the only developed country that discovered oil but saw lots of its people get poorer and fall into poverty. The *Herald* front page (28th April 2025) stated: "'Very deep poverty' now hits 80,000 young people" in Scotland. That disgrace is upon every adult's shoulder because with the energy resources we have the levels of poverty in our society should be impossible.

The present SNP attitude of treating our oil and gas as something to shut down as soon as possible is not followed anywhere else in the world. Whatever governments may say at the COP jamborees, many, including the big economy ones, do not practice the same in the world outside the conference halls.

China and India continue to build coal-fired power stations. Australia exports huge quantities of coal. Brazil is expanding its oil industry. Argentina is preparing to exploit its shale gas. Suriname is being investigated for oil. In the Eastern Mediterranean, Greece, Turkey and Cyprus have been arguing about who has law-of-the-sea possession over part of it because oil has been discovered and each of them would like to be the one to exploit it. Ghana has lately discovered oil and sees it as a game changer for economic development and improved the standard of living for its people. In Guyana (population 834,540), because of the oil discovered, the government sent each citizen over the age of eighteen a cheque for 100,000 Guyanese dollars from the oil bonus. With the average Guyanese annual wage at G$100,000, that is a full year's additional income. At the same time in energy-rich Scotland, old people had their winter fuel allowance cancelled and Scottish children are among the 50,000 deliberately pushed into poverty by the UK government. Are we Scots sane?

All other oil resource countries intend to keep producing, and that includes the United States, even under the Biden administration. Oil fuels 95 per cent of world transportation. As Deb Haaland, United States Secretary for the Interior in the Biden administration, said in August 2021: "Gas and oil production will continue well into the future. We believe that is the reality of our economy and the world in which we live." The world we live in will continue to use oil for energy and transport for a long time to come but it is also a vital feedstock for manufactures essential to the wellbeing of all humanity. Some 6,000 everyday essential products need oil in their creation. Among them are: solar panels, heart valves. eyeglasses, tires (without which electric cars will not run), vegan leather, dishwashing liquid, DVDs, and food preservatives, aspirin, antihistamines, antibacterials, suppositories, cough syrup, ointments, hand sanitiser, time release drugs, Vaseline, laxatives, sterile plastic bandages, disposable syringes gloves and masks, artificial limbs, hearing aids, bags and tubing used for analysis, along with soaps, insect repellents, clothes, dentures, lipstick, rugs, shampoo, and toothpaste. Oil is not going to be kept underground by other governments who have it or have found it.

In our devolution present, the SNP government and opposition can doge the oil issue. Devolution carries no responsibility for full fiscal judgements but dodging the big issues will not be possible with independence. Whatever the political colour of a post-independence government, armed with sovereign powers, it will need to muscle in on the oil industry as most other countries have done. When oil was discovered in Kuwait it was developed and owned by a British company. It had to get permission to drill and produce from the Kuwaiti government which had no knowledge of the industry and did not realise it was being stung when given 6p (old money) per barrel.

In Saudi Arabia, it was the Americans who found, drilled and produced. The then King, Abdul Aziz al Saud, was a clever man and a warrior, but was ignorant of what the oil could mean in terms of wealth. He got an annual lump sum bearing no relation to the value of the oil that had been discovered.

In Kuwait, Saudi Arabia, and the other gulf states, where the level of education, knowledge of the industry, and technical ability was low, an incredible level of exploitation of a country was the story at the start of their oil industry. But as the Arabs gained experience and more of their people were educated to the highest level, using their sovereign power, they demanded, and got, a bigger and bigger share of ownership of the oil, and eventually the lot.

The Saudi Arabia story and that of the Gulf Arabs in general – of original ignorance and evolution of knowledge leading to control – is encapsulated in the life of Ali Al-Naimi, who was a bare foot nomadic Bedouin child. His brother got a job as an office boy with ARAMCO, the giant US oil company in the Eastern Province of Saudi Arabia, and took young Ali with him to the school set up by the company. Ali then got a job as an office clerk but continued to study. He was one of its many citizens the Saudi government sent abroad to build an educated and technically qualified group capable of running things professionally. Ali went to Stanford University. When Saudi Arabia took full control of its oil industry Ali, by then highly skilled in understanding the international oil industry, became its President and CEO from 1983-1995 and then Minister for Petroleum and Mineral Resources from 1995-2016. From bare feet to being one of the most important men in the international energy industry.

The Scots do not have the low levels of education and technical know-how that was the case when oil began to flow from under the sand of Saudi Arabia, and yet we have allowed a massive amount of wealth to pass us by as though it wasn't worth bothering about. That is still the position we find ourselves in.

The use of sovereign power by an independent Scottish government to negotiate a share of ownership of the black stuff (either by some form of joint ownership, a wellhead tax, or a resource extraction tax) would not shock the oil companies. That has been their experience all over the world – first taking advantage of a nation with no knowledge of the industry, making huge profits while it remained ignorant, then giving way to its demands when it woke up. They must wonder in private how they have got away with it in Scotland in all these years since oil was first discovered.

I am not suggesting that Scotland, when independent, should seek to nationalise the whole of the North Sea and the Clair Field. It is a sad reality that we do not have the expertise to run and manage the oil industry in the international markets. In fact, the Scots are essentially ignorant about the oil industry, the quantities that are there, and how it is produced and distributed. If we were not so ignorant, we would not let happen what is happening now.

As a nation we know more about how our shipyards, steel mills and coal mines (all mostly redundant) operated than we do about the industry that has grown since the 1960s.

Remember the 2014 lie?

In 2014, Scots were told the North Sea had been so severely depleted that it was more a puddle than a reservoir and would hardly last another 20 years. No independent government, we were told, could rely upon it as a source of capital or revenue. Now that lie is being exposed by the very unionists who told it. New fields of oil and gas are celebrated and there are calls in the English press and from politicians at Westminster to produce it.

Chapter 8
Prepare now for Step Four to Independence

Step One to independence is building a winning vote. Step Two is demonstrating that vote by electorally forcing the UK government to concede a referendum where the question and organisation is set by the Scots, not Westminster. Step Three is winning the referendum.

But Scotland will not be independent when the result is announced. There will be another step, Step Four, a transition period ending with independence investing day, which the Scots can set, during which negotiations will be conducted between Scottish and English representatives. That will produce a treaty setting out the new relationship in areas such as trade, debt, free movement of people, reciprocal recognition of professional qualifications, food standards, division of assets and liabilities, dual-citizenship, and possibly defence. The Scots will also be involved in discussions with other states on related matters where we may or may not be seen as a continuing entity under various international legal instruments.

That is where Step Four becomes as important as the other three. The primary negotiations will be with England, our largest and most important "foreign" market, with which we have been entwined. These negotiations will determine the success or otherwise of an independent Scotland, at least in its first decade.

It is imperative that the detailed brief for Scotland's negotiators is well prepared before polling day. Those compiling the brief will need to ask difficult questions and find answers to them. It will be essential to define what are Scotland's strengths and weaknesses in our relationship with England, and theirs with us, and how those factors will shape the negotiations.

An example of the importance the negotiations will have is how they will affect the newly independent state's ability to set up its own currency, without which it cannot be truly sovereign. Setting up a currency is not difficult, as many post-colonial and post-Soviet Baltic states have shown, but certain matters are material to how successful it can be and these will emerge during negotiations.

The Scottish Currency Group and its Convener Dr. Tim Rideout have done a great deal of analysis and set out the need for work to be done now, including having a draft Bill ready to set up a Scottish Reserve Bank, well before even a referendum becomes possible, so that Scotland will not remain in the sterling zone a day longer than necessary.

Ahead of the 2021 Holyrood elections, when the SNP was still riding high, The Institute of Government published in April an excellent objective paper on the economic issues an independent Scottish government will need to address. Tony Mackay, the Scottish economist, published a critique but noted that it gave a "a good and balanced account of the Scottish economy" and contained "statistics and analysis... some people, such as SNP supporters, may disagree with." It was precisely that comment that drew me to the paper, because if we are to get our economic policies into a good shape, and make them convincing to the unionist voters we require, then we have to consider serious work that raises questions that need to be addressed.

Two things stood out for me on currency: that a new Scottish currency will have to be launched by a government and central bank "that have no track record in in adhering to fiscal discipline and price stability" – a new currency kid on the block for the international financial community to assess – and therefore how the new currency is constructed – floating, pegged, linked to another – along with the foreign exchange reserves available as its back, will determine its credibility.

The paper's estimate of foreign exchange reserves needed was $40bn but it also noted that if Scotland got only its proportionate share of UK reserves, that would only amount to $17bn, leaving a large shortfall and a question on credibility. Those were 2021 figures and no doubt will be different today but the imbalance between need and proportionate allocation is unlikely to have changed to Scottish advantage.

There will be many areas where the Scottish negotiating skills will be important, but none more so than on how much debt they are able to accept, the amount of foreign exchange reserves they can extract, and how those decisions will impact on the credibility of the new currency from which vital economic decisions will flow. Some time ago I spoke at two meetings. At both, to emphasise the trade-off nature of negotiations, I cited the foreign exchange reserves deficit.

"Let us," I said, "assume we are at the negotiation table. Across from us the English say they know we are going to be short on foreign exchange reserves, crucial for creating a credible currency, but they can help us bridge the gap. All we need do is give them a thirty-year lease on Faslane where they can continue to berth their Trident."

"What," I asked, "should be our reply?"

No one in those two rooms was prepared to give me an answer. "No Trident" has become a principle for the independence movement. For England, it will be among the most vital state interests. If any Scot believes Trident will not be one of the central issues in negotiations, with great pressure on the Scots to compromise, they don't yet know what realpolitik is – but they will when they sit down opposite an English side well-versed in this kind of bargaining.

The importance of the negotiations on currency is because credibility as seen internationally will be a test that must be passed, and central to that credibility is the level of debt Scotland will start with, as well as the amount of foreign-exchange reserves that Scots negotiators will extract from the UK Treasury in the negotiations.

Personally, I would start with saying Scotland should take no share of UK debt but negotiations to reach a successful outcome, where both sides have to be satisfied, will mean compromises. On some matters, the room for compromise will be narrow and that will have a knock-on effect on other issues.

If I was in charge of negotiations preparations, which I won't be, I would start now engaging our people in the negotiating equivalent to military war games, where proposals and counter-proposals are thrashed out to define the key demands each side is likely to make. Those composing the Scottish negotiations brief will have to see clearly what really matters to us in the Scottish-English relationship in all its aspects, and just what matters to the English in their relations with us. Where are the respective red lines beyond which neither side can go? In between them is the area of compromise.

Scotland's currency will be fiat money – that's why credibility matters

Until 1972, the world reserve currency was the US dollar linked to gold at $35 an ounce, with many other currencies then linked in turn to the dollar. In effect, a gold standard was based on a belief of all humankind throughout the ages, that gold has an intrinsic value. That is a puzzle. We cannot eat gold, it does not fuel our cars and planes, its main use is to make jewellery, and while it is employed in a variety of purposes such as electronics it can be substituted by palladium, platinum and silver. Yet in the human mind, gold has an intrinsic value that is indisputable.

Ever since that gold standard ceased to exist, all currencies are fiat ones. That is, pieces of paper with no link to anything we would regard as having an intrinsic value. We use them because we believe in them as a store of value and medium of exchange. That belief is based on nothing concrete. The day that we go into a shop and offer a £10-note for a piece of meat and the butcher has lost faith in its worth, there will be no meat in the basket. That shaky ground of belief is linked only to confidence in that piece of paper and when that goes, the currency is doomed. People in Zimbabwe know that only too well.

Governments which issue fiat currency can create and sustain belief and confidence in its worth by policy. The post-war German government did so for the D-Mark by its proclaimed fiscal and monetary discipline, which it could exercise in the context of a highly successful economic performance year after year. Scotland's government, when independent, will need to understand those basic factors and have them in place before issuing its own currency.

As well as those concerns, an independent government, when deciding to shift from the sterling currency transition stage, will need to take notice of the fact that all the transactions made by people in Scotland have been in sterling. Savings, mortgages, car loans, home and life insurance policies, company and private pension funds, credit card debt, and other things, are all and will be in sterling during the immediate post-independence phase.

Careful judgement will be needed not only regarding when to move to a Scottish currency, but what its relationship will continue to be with the pound sterling – the currency which will remain that of our most important trading partner.

Chapter 9
Why Independence is essential
Scotland in a world context

At my age, I have no politically active future and a limited time left as a citizen, but I am concerned about those who will be the people of Scotland in the long years ahead, in a world with greater challenges than faced my generation.

Over most of the twentieth century, the West of which we are part, commanded the international market place. Even when British, French and Dutch colonies had become politically free, they were not competitive. China was for a long time an economic basket case, reeling under the successive blunders unleashed by Mao Zedong. In 1975 Vietnam had just ended a devastating war, with the USA not lifting its economic embargo until 1994. India, although independent since 1948, was important geopolitically as a member of the non-aligned movement, standing aside from the US vs. USSR struggle, but was in economic terms a sleeping giant. Singapore was then a producer of cheap plastic toys. Much of Hong Kong's refugee population lived in shanty towns. In the early 1960s Gulf oil was less than $3 a barrel, only a small proportion of which went to the Arab states, with all of them many years away from modernity. We in the West were Kings of the world economy produced by the industrial revolution.

That easy-to-control-and-live-in world has gone. The power that lay in the Atlantic axis – the United States and Europe – has shifted to the Indo-Pacific. China and India are economic and political giants. Their colleges and universities are pouring out engineers and scientists. Vietnam is a new manufacturing power. Indonesia has new economic muscle. Singapore is an elite Asian success. Hong Kong is still a major financial sector. The Arab Gulf States are modern, have manufacturing capability, and are flexing their financial and diplomatic muscles in every area of the world. All of those countries are the West's equal and, in some areas, superior in the technological revolution now under way. As the *Economist* noted on 14th June 2024: whereas in the past "the West looked askance at the science coming out of China accusing it of mass-producing poor quality work... intellectual property thieves, rather than innovators. China is now a leading scientific power. Its scientists produce some the world's best research, particularly in chemistry, physics and material science... China's best universities are world class." In Africa, much slower to find lift-off than Asia, a young generation is emerging in a resource-rich continent.

It is in this new world that Scotland has to find its place. The question we must ask ourselves, and answer, is: "Are we equipped with the powers required to act decisively in our national interest in the new world order now emerging?" The answer is that without sovereignty, independence, we are not.

If we continue as a junior partner to England with not even a pinkie on the levers of power that matter, we face a future of going backwards. Not backwards for only some of us, but all of us.

*

Everyone in Scotland needs to recognise that and act upon it. There are two components to the reality. First, the Scottish Parliament and the Scottish Government, even if working efficiently, cannot alter the destiny of Scotland because they do not have the economic powers under devolution necessary to do so. Second, we are attached to a country that, due to its size and the economic levers it has, exerts a decisive effect on our economy.

I am aware of the argument that the SNP Scottish Government has not made effective use of the powers that it has in the devolution setting, and I don't contest it. Nor have I ever bought into the escape clause in the nationalist narrative that the manifest failures that is the record of the Sturgeon/Yousaf/Swinney governments are all due to wicked Westminster not handing over the cash. The Scottish Parliament's budget with the combination of grant and income tax is, in real terms, £60bn. The record of the past ten years is strewn with PR hype and failure to address priorities.

But even effective devolution would not address the salient weakness of the economic position Scotland is in: there is no control of a central bank that sets inflation targets and decides upon monetary policy, no influence on the fiscal policy measures creating or decreasing the level of demand in an economy to which we are attached, zero control of major resources such as oil and gas as well as the wind industry, and no control or even influence on trade access agreements to other markets.

Alex Salmond, in an astute political marketing exercise changed the name of the Holyrood administration from "Executive" to "Government," but a change of name does not change its powers or limitations. The Scottish Government is still only an Executive. The powers that were added by new Acts still has it reliant on the Barnett formula, and limited borrowing, with the new power to implement income tax levels proving to be more of a trap than a blessing.

There is a case short of independence – Devo-Max or quasi-federalism – that claims to include in its powers a number of the controls listed above that Holyrood does not have, but can have. This appears attractive as it seems to offer Government in the real sense of that word whilst Scotland remains in the Union. John Swinney, in the 2024 election, on ITV, confessed that he would support Devo-Max instead of gaining a second independence referendum. I shall address this proposal in a later chapter to demonstrate its inadequacy in the new world in which we must live.

Chapter 10
The Independence Movement
Sorting Out Our Historical and Current Relations with England

There is a body of people within the independence movement who deeply resent the senior-junior England-Scotland relationship. They see the 1707 Act of Union as a shotgun marriage, with Scotland treated as a colony of England ever since that fatal day of lost Scottish sovereignty.

I don't share that view. Very junior partner, yes. But colony? If Scotland was truly a colony, then the majority would not have voted as they did in 2014, for no colony given the opportunity of independence has ever refused it. The Scots aristocrats and the middle and upper classes were enthusiastic participants in the union because of the opportunities offered by accession to the English-British empire (two of Robert Burns' grandsons were with the East Indies Company). The empire and its growth in the industrial revolution was a mixed blessing for the Scottish working class. They were transferred from low paid agricultural work to highly skilled but still low paid work in new industries of steel making, shipbuilding, mining, and manufacturing in often squalid urban settings where diseases killed them and their children. A product of that period was the birth of the trade unions and, eventually, the Labour Party. These two organisations saw no difference between the interests and needs of Scottish, English and Welsh working classes.

Neither do I resent that the interests of England dominated and still dominate policy. The United Kingdom has always been the Kingdom of England with a Scottish appendage. That the Union was really England-continuing was widely recognised as de facto for almost three centuries. Only in recent years, within government and public media, has there been an avoidance of using "England" as synonymous with UK. Here are only a couple out of numerous examples to make this point. On 3rd September 1939, the headline in the Daily Express, with the largest circulation in the country, was "England Declares War," and Churchill in the first volume of his WWII memoir (published in 1948) notes that on 27th September 1938 while "the Fuehrer was at grips with his generals, Mr. Chamberlain himself was preparing to broadcast to the English nation." It never crossed Admiral Nelson's mind that his signal at Trafalgar of "England Expects," was anything other than a proper description of reality, despite having Scots captains in his fleet.

As I said, I don't resent this inevitable English domination of policy subsequent to the Act of Union, because resentment of that history takes us nowhere. Indeed, it is worse than that. Resentment at 1707 and all that has flowed from it has produced a paradox: many nationalists, and others who do not so identify, define themselves politically in relation to England. For the former England is the bane of Scottish life, while for the latter England is the cousin-neighbour whose hand is the one we must continue to hold. Even the adopted national anthem of Flower of Scotland is about our relations with England. All sides simply cannot shift it off. It is time we all did.

We need now to see our relationship with England in a different way, through the ice-cold concept of state interests.

What Scottish state interests tell us today is that our present subordinate status within the Union is a barrier to achieving the necessary, essential, control of our economy, and that only a clean political break from England will enable this nation to thrive and meet the formidable challenges in the new world order that is now evolving.

Chapter 11
Electoral Road and Referendum

There will be another referendum. The 2014 referendum was never a 'once in a generation' choice. It was an important event in a historic process in which Scotland's people have still to make the definitive decision on our relationship with others on the island of Great Britain.

Nationalists were upset, and seemed to think the Supreme Court in its 2022 judgment had ruled out another referendum forever, when all it did – as any first-year law student could have told the then First Minister – was to point out that the 1989 Act did not give the Scottish Parliament the legislative right to hold a referendum on independence. It did not, because it was not asked to, and could not, close the door on any future agreement between the Holyrood and Westminster Governments on holding another referendum.

Re-opening that door is the task of the movement. To do that we need to re-build, create policies that address our people's priority needs, and campaign to get the independence vote well above 55 per cent. We should be ambitious and aim for 60 per cent.

There are sound reasons for seeking that level. First is to put beyond doubt the legitimacy of the result when Yes wins. We should learn the lesson from the narrow victory of Leave in the Brexit vote, when people prominent among the losing side questioned the intelligence of those who voted Leave, suggested they did not really understand what they had voted for, and went on to seek a second vote. There continues to be a large section of people who opposed the decision to leave the EU who seek to show that Brexit does not work. We want a decisive result that makes that kind of conduct by the losing side impossible.

There is a second, profound, reason. If an independent Scotland is to achieve success, then the whole nation has to be positively involved in wanting that success – and that means those who lost contributing their talents and abilities to the national effort.

I now labour a point I have made before in these pages: the means to independence are as important in the long run as the end. How we campaign, how we treat those opposed to independence in the run-up and during the campaign will be a vital factor in how we bring the nation together after Yes wins. Getting people who did not vote for independence to work for its success, is not a matter of statesmanship for a few leaders, but for every individual in the Yes movement. Personal responsibility for how the campaign is conducted cannot be avoided by anyone.

Avoid a tactical error

A sign of the pathology to which I have referred is the argument from some, admittedly a minority, that we should abandon sending MPs to Westminster. While we are still in the unitary state of the UK, that is not sensible. Legislation and "events" there will have effect on Scotland, and our electors will find it difficult to accept that their interest is not registered where it matters.

Moreover, a presence at Westminster not only provides a legitimate platform from which to develop and state the case for independence, but it also provides links for our MPs to the international community through foreign embassies and the international media. This is of considerable value in getting our position better understood, and will have a bearing when, once more, we are engaged in extracting a referendum.

Chapter 12
The enhanced Vow: Ben Thomson's Home Rule

Quasi-Federalism
The best-of-both-worlds argument

In the next referendum there will be an element of Project Fear, but the real throw of the dice by the union will be to offer more powers to the Scottish parliament as Devo-Max, probably to be presented as Quasi-Federalism. The independence movement should be prepared for that. The trailer is already on the record, as is the failure of some in the movement to see it.

At the height of anxiety about the direction Scots were taking, as evidenced by the large SNP presence in the house of Commons at that time, the London based Constitutional Reform Group produced the Act of Union Bill in 2018, tabled in the House of Lords by Lord Lisvane (former chief clerk of the House of Commons). It was not meant to become an Act but to stimulate discussion, which it did, but only in English papers. It took until 3rd May 2021 for The *Scotsman* to publish an article by Lord Lisvane, which was read and then seemingly ignored.

Prominent Tory thinkers in England were also arguing for a federalist solution. None of them, it should be understood, were talking of federalising England, but simply of the relationship between Scotland and the rest of the UK.

Little notice was paid in Scotland to the thinking emerging in England. We were obsessively engaged with one thing – when there would be a second referendum.

Much more substantial than the Lisvane article was the publication by Birlinn in 2020 of Ben Thomson's book *Scottish Home Rule: the ANSWER to Scotland's CONSTITUTIONAL QUESTION* [the capitalisation is mine], which was more than an echo of the Vow-like promise made in 2014. I shall refer to the book hereafter as *Home Rule*. Chris Hanlon (The *National*, 5th January 2022) seemed to catch the English wind and the Devo-Max idea when he proposed a three-question referendum – independence, devo max, status quo – as a means of persuading the UK government to agree to a second referendum. A "something for everyone" solution. The lack of Scottish awareness of the thinking down in England, was evident from the eighty-eight comments that followed from his suggestion. Devo Max was denounced as nothing but another Vow hoax, and the tone was strident on the question being 'independence only.'

Those scornful activists writing in The *National* worked on instinct, not knowledge. Among the purposes of this book is to invite people in Scotland to discuss the respective merits of Scottish independence and the potential unionist alternative of Devo Max, on the basis that both are legitimate positions, with the ultimate conclusion being that independence and the ability to act free of control by others, is the superior choice.

The answer to home rule, devo-max and quasi-federalism

I spent a good part of 2019 and 2020 in drafting a political memoir, *A Difference of Opinion*, and saw it as bringing an end to a long political life. Then I read Ben Thomson's book, which had the merit of setting out in detail a quasi-federalist alternative to independence. As no one else was doing so, I decided to write a reply. But rising age drains energy and it has taken longer than I intended.

Whatever criticism I have about the case Ben Thomson puts, it is my earnest wish that those who favour independence read his book. I was taught by a self-educated generation of socialists in Ayrshire to always seek to understand where my opponents' ideas were coming from because, to my surprise, I might find some merit in them, and also some flaws in my own ideas. I pass on that bit of wisdom to my colleagues in the independence movement, and say that they will learn a great deal if they read and, among themselves, discuss what he says.

In my critique of *Home Rule*, I will not cover every detail of the new powers he proposes for the Scottish Parliament but concentrate on what I think most people would regard as the key ones by which we should measure the value of his quasi-federalism against independence.

When assessing his proposals, it should always be understood that no matter what advanced form devolution takes, it is a settlement that preserves one State – the UK – and in so doing preserves for the UK parliament the sole key sovereign role in political, economic and international matters that will always impact upon any devolved government.

Ben Thomson writes about the way forward as requiring "*a two-question referendum, which would allow voters to decide 'not only whether sovereignty should reside at either Holyrood or Westminster'... but whether or not they would prefer Home Rule – sovereignty* ***split*** *between two levels of government – to either of these options.*" (my emphasis)

Is his assertion that Home Rule – Devo Max will see sovereignty split between Scotland and the UK true? He obviously wishes it to be true, but it is not. Certainly, he would allocate to Holyrood a great raft of additional powers laid out in his Appendix III (which I set out a copy as the Appendix to this book), but there are among them important ones where the claim of a high degree of sovereignty is more than questionable.

One is "sea fishing" – important for key regions in Scotland. As the final negotiating hours over Brexit proved, because of historic rights, and recent ones, this is an international law issue which only the UK state can deal with because it is the only sovereign.

His additional powers include import and export control as well as the ability to vary or create new taxes. Small variations of taxes are one thing, but what about large ones or new taxes that would give Scotland a serious advantage over other parts of the UK in attracting investment, such as corporation tax abolished or set at, say, 10% when the UK was at 21%? I cannot see North East England and the rest of the UK agreeing to such sovereign powers for Scotland if its exercise could place them at such a disadvantage. If by export and import control, Scotland could have different customs duties than other parts of the UK, it is again difficult to see that being acceptable to England and Wales, or even workable, in a single market and custom union.

Monetary and fiscal policy, and management of the national debt are major economic levers, and when we come to them in Ben's book, the claim to split sovereignty within a Devo Max system falls down completely. Who is sole master of monetary policy, the national debt, and fiscal policy? It can only be the real sovereign, the British state.

Ben Thomson would seem to agree when unambiguously pointing out that in one State there can only be one monetary policy, one currency, and one central bank setting the rules on debt levels and interest rates. But then he wants, along with his Union cake, slices of a Scottish one too, arguing: "*This would not preclude there being a Scottish central bank, which could be responsible for financing any deficit that arises over expenditure in Scotland,* ***though this would have to be done within the overall framework of UK rules governing public expenditure.***" (emphasis added). Big bank, wee Bank – who will win? His idea of a Scottish Treasury hits the same non-sovereign problem for the Scottish side in Devo-Max.

Under Devo-Max, in a single currency area, Ben Thomson admits that a degree of coordination between the Scottish and UK treasuries would be required in order to reduce inconsistencies and ensure the fairness of both tax systems. Additionally, monetary and fiscal policy have an inescapable impact on each other; the UK Treasury could not avoid oversight of the Scottish Treasury to ensure its policies were consistent with UK-wide monetary policy. When Ben Thomson uses words such as "coordination," "inconsistencies," "monitored," "input," as he does to describe the Scottish-UK Treasuries' relationship, they cannot disguise the truth: the UK would be the superior in regard to control of monetary policy and so would be doing the monitoring and providing the input to Scottish policy.

Taking into account the respective weights of each Treasury, like the banks it would be the wee one against the big one if any dispute arose and given the power the big one would have, it would be no contest.

The more one reads the exposition in *Home Rule*, the less plausible is the idea that sovereignty, a term meaning total control, is involved. Note the "within limits" caveat inserted in the string of economic powers the author wants to come our way: "powers to raise taxes and borrow within limits to meet Scottish experience, financial services, financial markets and money laundering." Who would set the limits? The Treasury of the United Kingdom, responsible to the UK parliament, the only sovereign.

This limitation appears again and again. The Scottish government "would have control over the allocation of resources' drawn from its taxing powers" but "its public spending would have to adhere to rules on overall public expenditure set at UK level."

But fiscal policy is not formed in a vacuum. Its purpose is both to act on demand in an economy and to meet public expenditure responsibilities. Some of the most important of the latter arise from the existence of the welfare state, and while the NHS is presently devolved, that is not wholly the case with social security provision.

The 2016 Act gave the Scottish government eleven social security powers. Included within *Ill-Health and Disability* are – Disability Living Allowance, Personal Independence Payments, Severe Disablement Allowance, Industrial Injuries Disablement Benefit, and Attendance Allowance. There are also the Carer's Allowance, Sure Start Maternity Grant, and Discretionary Housing Payments.

In other welfare state areas, the UK funds and sets levels of payment on Universal Credit, Jobseeker's Allowance, Child Benefit, and the state pension. These are not minor items, and form an important component of fiscal policy in Scotland, over which the Scottish parliament at present has no control. Given the costs involved in Universal Credit and other benefits funded directly by the UK, that central government is unlikely to cede control pf them even in a Devo-Max constitutional arrangement.

Ben Thomson says that the policies to promote the welfare state's aim of "social protection and poverty alleviation" are best set and manged by the government body nearest to the problems, and so there should be a full transfer of control over the whole range of payments, including the state pension. By "control" I have assumed, I think fairly, that he means raising the cash through Scottish-based taxation as well as the distribution of benefits. However, if I read him correctly, he seems to anticipate that there may be a shortfall in Scottish income from internal taxation, and to meet this he advocates a UK "Social Cohesion Fund" from which income gaps in Scotland could be plugged. That is an admission of the limits *Home Rule* would impose upon a Scottish government: limits that cannot be reconciled by any claim to a split of sovereignty.

There is a fatal ambiguity about sovereignty in *Home Rule.* In one passage it will be "split," between Scotland and the UK, while in another it is "shared." This is not a matter of semantics. There is a significant difference between "split' and "shared." Split means a sharp defined division, where there can be no mistake that the sovereignty held by each partner is theirs in absolute terms. The examples above, in the case of economic powers, where limits will be imposed on Scotland's fiscal autonomy, demonstrate that there is no split of sovereignty.

The concept of "shared" is different from that of "split." Shared requires an undisputed central legal authority, above those who are doing the sharing, applying its acquired shared-power over all parts of the whole, otherwise the shared arrangement could not work. A new body superior to the House of Commons? Not something likely to be accepted by that key institution.

The European Union presents a good example of the difference between "split" and "shared." Where it is split, that is where member states retain their individual sovereignty in certain areas: Germany could and did do a deal with Russia to supply gas via the Nord Stream 2 pipeline despite concerns of its EU neighbours, and then undid it as a consequence of Russia's invasion of Ukraine. It might go back to the original agreement in future. That is Germany's sovereign right. But where Germany and other EU members "share" their sovereignty, as in the Eurozone, that can only work with a single monetary authority – the European Central Bank – whose decisions are binding on all.

I criticise Ben Thomson for lack of clarity between split and shared but I doubt if anyone in the leadership of the SNP has given any thought to the important differences, the resolution of which will eventually decide the final form the European Union takes. Perhaps before they attempt to take us back into the EU, they will set before the Scottish people what sovereignty they will split with Brussels and which portions they will share. It would be worthwhile for the SNP to talk to the Greeks, who will be able to explain that they found the "shared" sovereignty that created the euro and produced a central authority with the power to crush their economy, an experience from which they are only now recovering.

***Home Rule's* view of a written constitution:** For Devo-Max to work, its author argues, the relationship between Scotland and the UK must be enshrined in a written constitution. Having pinned its whole case on that "must", it begs the question of whether constructing a written constitution for what he admits is an asymmetric system would be achievable and what its legal status would be?

It is difficult to see how Ben Thomson's written constitution, however well crafted, and however many of the bits of the present one it incorporated, could become anything but the fundamental law sovereign law governing the whole of the United Kingdom – and thus specifically declare that it was replacing the sovereignty of Parliament. In any construction of Home Rule/Devo Max, the English view on this would be decisive. It is by no means certain, and highly unlikely, that they would agree with a written document replacing the sovereignty of the Westminster Parliament, the latter an entrenched constitutional principle in the English mind.

One of the arguments I have heard from English scholars over the years in favour of the present constitution is its elasticity: the ability to accommodate new circumstances and bring them smoothly into the constitution as natural developments. They see this, as distinct from the black and white lettering of a written document, as a blessing the past has endowed upon the present and future. I cannot find in my monitoring of English opinion, any enthusiasm for removing the sovereignty of parliament and replacing it with what they would regard as a piece of paper.

To sum up: as a Devo-Max enthusiast, Ben Thomson cannot escape from the fact that inherent in devolution are the limitations on a Scottish Parliament as identified in this chapter. It is understandable that in his presentation he emphasises the positives in terms of the transfer of substantial powers to Holyrood but he should be more open about the serious limitations that accompany them. He and Devo-Max supporters should be prepared to tell people these limitations are a price worth paying to remain within the UK. That would be a more honest stance than to pretend that there is an actual transfer of sovereignty in what is being offered.

Those of us who favour independence recognise that the limitations on Scotland in a devolution settlement are due, as Paul Scott once put it, to being in bed with an English elephant. If we stay in that bed, no matter how we shift bedclothes around, the elephant will always dominate. No matter the form and substance of any devolution proposal, it will not be possible for the Scottish people to create an economy that is designed to prioritise what is best for us without being macro-controlled and "monitored" by a large neighbour with legal rights over us.

Scotland having and exercising sovereignty is compatible with a policy of co-operation with others

Ben Thomson writes about sovereignty and how, to back up his case, it can be divided. Yet he doesn't really have much time for it:

He may be correct about young people but there is nothing vague or antiquated about sovereignty. It represents the power of a national unit to exercise its own judgement in its own affairs and how it decides to relate to other States. Not all nations are States: the Kurds, Basques, Catalans and we Scots are but some examples. But where nations are sovereign, in most of this world (members of the European Union being an exception), they hold on to it. Even there, they have not yet given it all up.

There is a school of thought, that in this interconnected world of trade, business and multilateral organisations such as the United Nations, IMF, World Bank, WTO, WHO, G7 and G20, ASEAN, BRICS, TPP, the idea of the nation state and its twin – the concept of sovereignty – is old hat, no longer relevant, and a foolish notion based on nostalgia for long ago times. That is a genuinely held and often expressed belief.

Those of that view can cite international organisations where States meet and accept decisions made by consensus (WTO) or votes (United Nations General Assembly and the Security Council), but it is a sovereign decision to join them, and no sovereign nation State can be made to join them by others. It would be an act of self-harm to leave them, but a sovereign State could do so and none could stop them. The United States is an example of a country that exercises its sovereignty to leave and re-join international organisations, as it has done with UNESCO – leaving under Reagan in 1984, re-joined by Clinton 1997, left by Trump in 2019, with Joe Biden in 2021 going back in, before it was taken out again by Trump.

All sovereign nation States have border controls, most have their own currency, own defence policy, and it is their sole decision on whether or not to join with others in trade and other arrangements.

As for young people, it is clear that they are fired by idealism and enthusiasm for international organisations that have a global importance: the European Court of Human Rights, the International Court of Justice, the International Criminal Court, and the Paris Agreement on climate. Whether their youthful views on life and sovereignty will change in time is a moot point. Many former Trotskyists were prominent in Tony Blair's cabinet and government, including the man himself in his student days. By the time they reached the cabinet they were not Marxists, not even Labour, but New Labour, which some others outside the Blair circle construed as Not Labour.

What is not a moot point is that in each of the organisations mentioned above, the exercise of State sovereign power is there for all to see. The European Convention on Human Rights upon which the Strasbourg Court adjudicates applies to states just as so long as they decide to remain within it. They have the sovereign ability to leave and not to comply with judgements (I believe Scotland should remain in the ECHR).

There have been many examples of states refusing to appear before the ICJ even when it has declared it had jurisdiction. Iran refused to appear when the USA took it there over diplomats taken as hostages in 1979; the same USA refused to appear when Nicaragua took it to the court over the mining of its harbours. Recently, the Philippines a signatory, took China, a non-signatory, to the ICJ over rights in the South China Sea. ICJ declaration of jurisdiction on the matter, and its decision in favour of the Philippines, made no difference to China who ignored the decision.

The United States, China, Russia, India, Pakistan, Vietnam, Thailand, and Singapore do not recognise the jurisdiction of the International Criminal Court. And while China, India and African countries are signatories to the Paris agreement, they used their sovereign power to keep it just that, an agreement, not a Treaty to which they would be legally bound. In exercising sovereignty African states are planning to build 1,260 new coal-fired power stations, India intends to build 300, China 800, and Japan has announced 30.

These coal-fired exercises in sovereignty, despite the Paris Agreement and the annual COPs declarations, drive home the reality that sovereignty exists and is regarded as essential to a country's independence, a view shared by the majority of States.

*

Ben Thomson himself provides examples, unaware that he undermines his own case, and unwittingly emphasises that for independence. He cites Iceland and Greece. The first is a fully independent country with its own currency, while Greece, without its own currency, is entwined in the multi-member eurozone.

He points to the difference between the two in the handling of the financial crash in 2007-8. Iceland suffered bankrupt banks, a fall in GDP by 40%, a stock market crash of 90%, and the krona fell 50% against the US dollar. Half the country's wealth was wiped out. The government was forced into capital controls.

Yet, as he explains, Iceland's independence and own currency was its salvation. Its economy recovered because the devalued currency made its exports cheaper, and with its devalued assets it was more able than most in successfully attracting a flow of inward investment. The result: today, there is strong economic growth with a GDP higher than before the crisis. The key here was that Iceland, fully sovereign, could act in its own interests, reliant on no other power centre exercising sovereign control over its decisions.

It may be recalled that Prime Minister Gordon Brown, in a spat with Iceland at that time, a minnow compared to the UK, sought to control that nation and punish it for its independent actions, by using one of the UK's terrorism acts. Iceland saw him off.

The case with Greece's handling of the crisis was very different. It was not fully sovereign, having shed what Iceland kept – its own currency. Greece had to do what the EU Troika told it to as the price of gaining access to what might be called a cohesion fund. The price: unemployment at 26%, a fall in GDP per head of 40%, long standing employment protection laws torn up, and a fire sale of State assets. No Greek separate currency, no devaluation to make it more competitive against other European countries in the single monetary zone, no way out of social purgatory. It has taken long painful years for Greece to recover from that pummelling. The Greek-Iceland lesson is that sovereignty matters – not split, not shared, but full.

Polls asking the wrong question

Every now and again, we find an opinion poll telling us the ups and downs of the percentage for and against independence. But the question is just exactly that, as though there is no other more relevant choice. The pollsters are asking the wrong question. The correct one would be Independence vs. Devo-Max. I hope it is posed, as it would do much to jolt the independence movement into a proper understanding of Scottish opinion on the constitution, and start the debate we must have long before we are finally asked to choose between them in a real poll.

Chapter 13
Foreign and Defence Policy

No form of devolution at whatever level can transfer control of foreign and defence policy from London to Edinburgh. It does not follow even after all the years that Scotland has been part of the UK, that Scotland's foreign policy interests are, and will be, exactly the same as England's on every issue. There was a very sharp division of opinion over the UK's invasion of Iraq, as demonstrated by the huge demonstration against it in Glasgow, drawn from all parties and people of no party, and it is arguable that UK intervention in Libya was an action Scots would not have found sensible – that is if it had been discussed here. The UK is still influenced by its imperial past, as is manifest in its expressed desire to remain a global player in world affairs, despite its economic decline and its consequent fall from a first to a second-tier military power, with an enormous difference in hard power clout between those two categories.

The question for people in Scotland is whether we are content to be drawn along in the wake of a second rank England-UK, or whether, as a small independent nation, we can look after ourselves and thus make a better contribution to the international community than as a silent witness to whatever Westminster decides?

When it comes to foreign and defence policy, which are inextricably linked, small nations must make a choice: they either opt for neutrality or seek alliances with powers greater than themselves while at the same time seeking to retain an ability to act differently from the principal ally, if that is deemed essential to their national interest. The choice, and the degree of flexibility available, is dictated by geography, lessons of history, and interpretation of geopolitical shifts in power.

The Scandinavian and Baltic countries present good examples. Denmark is a longstanding member of NATO and the EU. Norway only of NATO. Finland and Sweden, also in the EU, were never in NATO because as a Swedish diplomat told me years ago, joining NATO would be construed by its then neighbour the USSR as an unfriendly act. However, after the Russian invasion of Ukraine in February 2022, re-assessment of the power balance in Europe saw both Finland and Sweden joining NATO as a better insurance policy than neutrality.

The Baltic states of Lithuania, Estonia and Latvia, which extracted themselves from the Soviet Union, with the latter two having large numbers of ethnic Russians in their populations (Latvia 24.9%, Estonia 24.8%), not only joined the EU, but also NATO, and so provided themselves a shield against their large and not very friendly neighbour, thus offsetting the fact of geography.

On the other side of the world New Zealand, seen as an American ally, one of the Five Eyes intelligence network (US, UK, Canada, Australia, New Zealand) refused in January 2021 to sign a joint declaration criticising China. With 40 per cent of its exports going to China, and being a small export orientated State, it did not think a signature was in its national interests.

In the history of the Union, Scots have been Prime Minster, Foreign Secretary, and Commonwealth

Secretary, and we have even had a Scot as secretary general of NATO. Yet foreign policy does not command a great deal of time in our political debates in Scotland, nor does the subject of foreign policy as distinct from reporting on foreign countries take up much space in our newspapers and other media outlets. David Pratt in The *Herald* is an exception.

We had 56 SNP MPs at one time, and still have MPs in the House of Commons. There are Scottish peers in the Lords. When last was a speech, or an in-depth article on wide foreign policy issues (as distinct from comment on Ukraine) by any of them, published in the Scottish press? There is no editorial injunction against reporting, or publishing an MP's, or a Lord's speech or articles, yet it is difficult to find any.

There are exceptions. Stewart Macdonald MP wrote regularly in The Scotsman. Stephen Gethins, ex-MP, now MP again, published *Nation to Nation: Scotland's Place in the World in* 2020, and now writes regularly. But where are the others?

On MPs especially, rests a duty to assist the public to get the deepest possible understanding of international, economic, foreign and defence policy issues and this can only be done by writing articles for newspapers and other media outlets as well as speaking inside and outside of Parliament. News organisations have researchers and the House of Commons library is one of the best sources of information to be found anywhere in the world. MPs have an educational role, but do not practice it in foreign and defence policy. Their role is not much better in the area of economics.

Foreign policy and its concomitant, defence, has a low priority in the constitutional debate, as low on the independence side as on the unionist one. This may be because the magnet of attention in Scottish politics is the Edinburgh Parliament, whose remit is domestic. For Scots, when defence issues emerge, it is whether the MOD will order warships for Yarrow's on the Clyde, or the regular denunciation of Trident by the SNP.

That Westminster layer above us, where foreign affairs and defence is reserved to the UK government and parliament, has meant that over the years the Scots leave "big" issues to others; even when it is a Scot in charge, he works within the Whitehall circle, with little feed-back to those of us up here. The result is a parochial Scotland.

Some might hold the view that "It would be foolish to argue that an independent Scotland would bring anything remarkably new to the world community." Those words, and their meaning, fit nicely into the image of Scotland that some of my fellow citizens have: that we have to hold the hand of big cousin England to count for anything. Harsh? Not really. We are a remarkable nation, probably unique, in that we have citizens who think we are not able to run our own affairs. I have met them.

Independence in foreign policy will bring to Scotland its value of responsible engagement with other sovereign powers. We would have a diplomatic service, debates about where to locate our embassies, seeking to strike a balance between those we saw as only of interest for trade, and those we regard as politically important such as what position on issues we would take in the UN General Assembly and other international organisations. There would be foreign office questions in parliament and foreign affairs debates. In short, as a regular occurrence, the people of Scotland and those they elect would be required to think well beyond the narrow boundaries that hedge us in at present. Independence offers an engagement with the world that no form of devolution ever can.

As a member of NATO, Scotland would be in a higher league of defence and foreign policy – one we cannot enter at present. We would be forced into a sharp learning curve, because NATO is more than a military alliance. It is also political. Headed by a civilian, it has six political divisions, and each member state is represented by an ambassador and it has external relations with states not in NATO. It has a military structure but operates under a civilian umbrella. It has been grounded on Western and Central Europe's relationship with the United States, something that can no longer be taken for granted given the Trump doctrine of America First, raising the probability that a purely European-led NATO will emerge. Engagement in NATO will require us to think much deeper and wider than ever before. Ben Thomson's *Home Rule*, instead, would keep us locked up in a domestic cage, with foreign and defence policy staying where it is now, in Westminster.

While the US remains the most powerful State in the world, has a nuclear weapons capacity to obliterate humankind, and sits on 800 military bases in 81 countries, all is not as it appears. Its military is over-stretched. It is failing to meet its recruitment numbers. Many who are recruited are not in good physical condition. Its weapon-making industrial capacity is a shadow of its former strength. Its budget has a deficit of $1.6 trillion (that will get bigger), a national debt of $36 trillion and rising, meaning it has to borrow on the international financial markets and thereby pay more debt interest than it spends on defence. Whether by January 2029 (when his presidency ends),

President Trump's internal and external policies will have combined to make America great again, or are delusional and will make America decline and fatally weaken the dollar's status as the world reserve currency, is one of the interesting questions of our times.

Conservative writers have been expressing concern about America's military capacity, and Holman W Jenkins, a leading columnist, on 5th March 2025, drew attention to "China's strategic bet that the US is on a path of inexorable fiscal decline."

From the time of Nixon's turn towards China in the early 1970s, the United States has increasingly seen its principal national interests from the standpoint of an Asia-Pacific power. It is instructive that on 14th February 2022, a day when the Ukraine crisis was supposedly reaching its climax, the *Wall Street Journal* chose to publish an opinion piece by Elbridge Colby of the Marathon Initiative, under the title "The Strategy of Denial: American Defence in an Age of Great Power Conflict":

Denying China the ability to dominate Asia is more important than anything that happens in Europe. To be blunt: Taiwan is more important than Ukraine.

Mr. Colby was confirmed by the Senate in 2025 as Under Secretary for Policy in the US Defence Department. His identification of where US interests really lie, shows the importance of NATO's European members considering change on "who leads" between them and the United States within the alliance, and any conclusions reached will be important for Scotland's security. But without independence, we shall have no role or voice in the matter.

*

The assumption I make about Scotland as a member of NATO will be contested by CND and many in the SNP and wider movement, but not I believe by the people. There is always a touch of anti-American attitude in Scotland, based on dislike of some of the actions the US has taken as the superpower. I suspect that dislike will intensify during the Trump presidency. That will not last forever, but will leave a legacy of doubt about Atlantic relations.

I have always opposed the retention of nuclear weapons by the United Kingdom, and their possession by others, and therefore also opposed the use of Faslane as the base for them. Annihilation of millions of people, who have never met each other, as a result of failure in the exercise of wisdom, can only happen when we empty the human universe of its moral content. We are not yet in that position, and the idealist in me struggles to hold fast to the moral case against the H-Bomb and its successors, while at the same time facing the fact that nuclear weapons are part and parcel of the necessary alliances we are in.

There is another reason divorced from the moral argument for opposing UK retention of its submarine-based nuclear weapons. The Trident delivery system is not British, but leased from the United States and its maintenance carried out by the United States. It is not, therefore, genuinely independent. It is costly, and the consequence of its call on expenditure has degraded the lethal power of the conventional armed forces. But for a second-rank country, even with those limitations and consequences, holding on to it is the defence priority.

Along with the SNP conference that reversed its anti-NATO stance prior to the 2014 referendum, I recognise that our geography places us in the sphere of influence of the major western nuclear power, and also that of the European members of NATO, a circumstance that will compel us to remain in the alliance. We Scots are in the world that is, not the world as we might like it to be. None of us can ignore one of the lessons of the Ukraine-Russia war: that the nuclear power – Russi -, and its threat to use its weapons, had a significant effect on the decision of Biden and a number of European leaders to put restrictions on how Ukraine could use the weapons supplied to it. That "Russian nuclear threat" to non-nuclear Ukraine has reinforced the UK government view, and I suspect that of the people here as well as in England, on the necessity to retain Trident. It has not gone unnoticed around the world that had Ukraine kept its nuclear weapons on gaining independence instead of surrendering them to Russia for paper guarantees of security that have proved worthless, President Zelensky and his country would not be dismissively described by President Trump as having "no cards to play."

Being in NATO does not lock Scotland out of relations with the rest of the world in political, economic and trade relations. Most countries in the world are outside of Europe, as are most of the world's people. Different regions present different problems and opportunities in the development of foreign policy, and trade, in which membership of NATO will have little or no bearing.

Foreign policy is important for small as well as for big nations
Why an independent Scotland can be relevant

We are in an era of enormous change in the power balance of the world. Such an event has not been experienced for more than three hundred years. One epoch has ended, and another has begun. Within the reasons for it lies the question of whether the Thucydides trap will bring earth shattering conflict between the waning world power USA and the rising power of China.

Whether we are citizens of small or large nation, for once it is true that we are all in it together. Understanding of what has happened is required if this tectonic shift in world affairs is to be managed successfully.

Enquiring, thinking, and discussing by and among many people, from all countries, of all sizes, will be needed if the problems and dangers inherent in this change are to be managed differently from the past epochs, in which humanity was afflicted with wars of organised unsurpassed savagery. In the early years of the 20th century in the last epoch, power came out of the barrel of a machine gun, and ended in later years with the nuclear weapon. The new epoch starts with nuclear weapons in the armoury of eight States and the knowledge of how to build them widespread among others.

Those who sit in the leadership of great powers, along with second-ranking powers, will inevitably play their part in forming a new world order. State interests will influence their thinking, as will the power they are able to deploy. Moreover, those first- and second-ranking states will be active in a heterogeneous world, one with no common philosophy, ideology or set of values; they will have suspicions about each other, and interests will clash over resources.

It is in that setting small nations have an important role. They may have successful economies, but that success does not translate into great political or military power and so they pose no threat to the great- and middle-ranking powers. They can act and articulate their views in the world forum in a way that commands attention of the great and near-great, and make a valuable contribution to the building of international institutions designed to limit the potential for friction to become conflict. And individuals from small nations can have worldwide influence and impact. The Scottish Enlightenment has been one such in world affairs.

Hume on philosophy and Adam Smith on economics helped make the world we have today. It is little remarked upon in Scotland that the works of those philosophers of the Scottish Enlightenment, especially Hume and Adam Smith, had a profound effect on the authors of the Federalist papers and the US constitution, such as Madison and Hamilton; moreover, Abraham Lincoln was influenced by the works of Robert Burns. So important was Burns in the lives of the Lincolns, that Mrs. Lincoln made a special visit to Burns Cottage in Alloway after the death of her husband.

Yes, I know, before I am pounced upon: those Enlightenment giants lived within the United Kingdom, and didn't need an independent Scotland as a necessary condition for the thinking and writing that helped transform the West from a society shackled by superstition to one in which rational thought let loose the human capacity for intellectual adventure – with the scientific, social and political benefits that flowed from it. But their massive influence on Western thought is not entitled the "United Kingdom Enlightenment," but the Scottish Enlightenment, because it was from that little part of the world that individuals brought forth great works, not as a result of union or empire, but from a nation with its own distinct view based on its own distinctive educated body of thought.

In future, Scots as individuals or in groups, may or may not produce ideas on how the world might improve present international institutions, or build new ones that would guide the human family onto a peaceful road. I freely admit they could do it in a devolution setting. But, the record of non-participation in international affairs, in any serious way, after twenty-six years of Holyrood narrowing our horizons, shows that we are likely to remain non-participants in world affairs.

We are more likely to enter the big thinking arena if we are independent and a participating part of the international community at the United Nations and other organisations open only to states.

*

My view of the profound change in the balance of power in the world, is shared by many others, but not by all. In his book *The Ambassadors: Thinking about Diplomacy from Richelieu to Modern Times*, Robert Cooper, armed with great experience in diplomacy, believes the western-created system is still the centrepiece of today's world because of its power. Others believe he is mistaken.

Roberts and others who think that the fundamentals of the current western-built international system may be a bit ragged but are still essentially intact, do of course recognise the "China problem" and the developments taking place in Asia. But they can point to current facts of economic and military power to support their position. China and India are examples of fast developing states, and the former has made spectacular progress. But look at the facts, they say.

Cooper cited 2019 data. China's GDP per capita was $16,117, and India $6,700, whereas the USA was $62,530, Germany $53,919, UK $46,359, and France $46,200. Together the EU27 and USA traded 42% of world exports and 43% of imports. Indisputably, Western states are still well ahead in terms of prosperity and the technical level of their economies. The USA combined with NATO outranks, in decisive destructive military power, all potential adversaries put together. China can boast about its achievement but Xi Jinping set the ambition for his country no higher than becoming a "moderately prosperous" nation.

Those who view things that way are not complacent. They are aware of China's ambitions, and India's, but argue that the way to block, or more realistically, restrain China's power, is for Western nations to ally with democratic states and others in the Indo-Pacific region. A by-product of that geopolitical policy would be to lock parts of Asia into what would still be a world order based on how the West constructed it. Even if I am right and the sceptics are wrong about the epochal change driving the Indo-Pacific region upwards and onwards, that policy is one that will need to be considered as the West and China's near neighbours, work out what to do about China.

However, I think a short look at history might reinforce my argument about a massive shift in power underway. Western hegemony did not materialise all at once; it gathered momentum, as is happening with countries in the Indo-Pacific. Not recognising world-shaping change does not stop it happening, as the Chinese Imperial rulers in the past learnt to their cost.

In 1793, when Lord Macartney made the first British diplomatic visit to China, it was to a great political and economic power that was producing 35% of world GDP, far greater than any country in the West – whose industrial revolution was just getting underway. The new power centres developing were not obvious. Lord Macartney was expected to kowtow to the Emperor Qianlong – nine kneeling bows – which he refused to do. Down on one knee and lowered head, was as far as he would go, exactly, he explained, what he did before the "King of England."

Qianlong was not pleased: "When foreigners come seeking audience with me and are sincere and submissive, then I always treat them with kindness, but if they come in arrogance they get nothing" (a bit like superpower Trump and his tariffs today). He was far from impressed by the British goods shown to him: "I do not need your manufactures." In 1840, only 47 years later from that dismissive response, those manufactures in the form of Royal Navy ships and modern guns smashed China's war junks in an unequal battle, to win the first opium war and start the long humiliation of the Middle Kingdom.

States from different regions of the world have been dominant at different times. Powers have risen, waned and fallen. None, it appears, can escape that cycle.

What we call the West, or what I think more accurately, the Atlantic axis of Europe and the USA, was becoming the dominant force from the mid eighteenth century when its industrial revolution brought new technologies, new energies, new ambitions, in every area of economic and political policy and, inevitability, superior military power.

From then on, the rest of the world was subject either to direct or indirect control by Western powers as their colonial appetite grew. In the 20th century, western hegemony was challenged ideologically by the communist movement led by the Soviet Union, with China a minor player by comparison due to its slow, painful recovery from the 1935-49 war. However, even with its emergence as a great power post-1945, the USSR and its imperial holdings in Eastern Europe, did not displace, or seriously dent, Western dominance. They could never compete economically.

For a good part of the twentieth century Central and Latin America were under effective control of the United States, the UK's empire was intact, as was that of France and the Netherlands. The results of the 1884-85 Berlin conference of European Statesmen that carved up Africa did not change.

The framework of economic, diplomatic, and military power that sustained Western control began to be dismantled by the steady loss of imperial possessions by Britain, France and the Dutch in the second half of the twentieth century, leaving the USA as the post-war inheritor of dominance. But the USA too, once the world's great creditor, and now its biggest debtor, is finding that it is no longer a king pin with the world doing its bidding. The West's turn in the cycle is over. The Indo-Pacific time has come.

How do Western nations handle this cycle of change? How do we handle the specific problem of China's geopolitical reach into areas previously within our singular sphere of influence, not simply because of its growing economic power, but the export of its authoritarian ideas and the systems they create?

For centuries western powers regarded it as a right to build and sail blue water fleets into Asian, African and Latin American waters, declaring maritime areas thousands of miles away from their home bases as of their national interest. Even today HMS Prince of Wales headed for the South China Sea, as though there has been no change in the West-China power balance. So, how will the West react when China sails its aircraft carrier group up our west coast Atlantic waters towards the Arctic, all in international waters? When Russia sends its warships through the English Channel, the MOD and media reaction is as though it has no right to do so, and is being provocative. How does the West handle itself in a new international community in which many in Asia do not accept as universal the values we proclaim to be so?

*

The United States' post-1945 empire was different from all others before it. It exerted its power in countries without formally occupying them, with the Philippines and some small Pacific islands being exceptions. Now China is following the same path, as Sri Lanka and African states are discovering when, unable to service the Chinese loans to build a port in Sri Lanka or exploit ores in Africa, they find the Chinese taking over ownership. Does the West sit back and watch helplessly as the Belt and Road rolls on or instead seek to find answers?

More often now, it is not China and its people that Western politicians and thinkers refer to but the Chinese Communist Party. That distinction is not meant to indicate that there is a significant gap between the Chinese people and the party that governs them. It simply recognises that the CCP and its leadership is China for all practical purposes in our dealings with it.

Have Scotland's people anything to contribute to Western policy on China, or towards other Asian powers?

Ideas from every Western nation, large and small, are needed. The reason for the importance of ideas, is that the CCP is not open to the type of pressures that would work with a lesser power – trade sanctions, cut-off from financial markets, and being frozen out of international organisations. Trump's first administration struck at the CCP with both tariffs and blocking of technology companies, but there was no evidence that it made any difference to CCP policy at that time. As I write in July 2025, Trump in his second term is going much further, this time using tariff negotiations with other countries to build an economic bloc with the aim of isolating China. That strategy is based on Trump's belief that America's self-perceived world dominance means it can ignore the state interests of others. I think he is more likely to be today's Qianlong, blind to new power centres arising in Asia and other parts of the world.

*

As I have noted above, one policy proposal is available: the creation of political partnerships with other democracies, and others like Vietnam who have historical cause to be concerned about China. But that is a defensive posture, which implicitly recognises that there is no policy that, when applied to the CCP, creates a cost it may think not worth paying. Even if a Western-Indo-Pacific political partnership is formed, it is unlikely to become also a military one, as none of those involved will want to stumble into a military problem with the CCP.

So, as well as adjusting to the rise of the Indo-Pacific nations and its effect of relegating Western power, there is the CCP problem. Intelligent thinking, not the rattling of hardware, is what will be at a premium in

Western circles as we grapple with our China relations. Whether that thinking comes from large or small nations will not matter. Do Scots want to take part or are we content to let others do the thinking?

To answer that, we need to decide where we want our place to be in the new unstable world order. Is it possible to stimulate sufficient interest in such globally important issues when Ben Thomson's *Home Rule* system puts emphasis on just that – home affairs. I believe that the stark difference that sovereignty holds compared to Devo-Max is the more likely to make us think on that higher level.

Chapter 14
The Scottish Parliament

High time it was submitted to examination
And so too our electoral system

If an independent Scotland is to be a success, a lot will depend on how the new sovereign parliament goes about its business as a legislature, and how effective the executive performs. There are lessons to be learned for a future independent parliament from the present devolved one.

Academics have, as one would expect, looked critically at how the Scottish parliament has given effect to the 1998 and subsequent Acts. But little, if anything, of their work has come to the notice of the citizenry.

It is twenty-six years since the opening of the Scottish Parliament. There was a great deal of hope about how it would make a real difference to our society, based on the oft-repeated belief it would be very different from Westminster. The chamber of the Parliament was designed to help make it a less confrontational forum. I never bought into that view. The development of Scottish political life marched hand in hand with that in England and Wales, and the clash of party and class interests has played a large part on why we have adversarial politics. To believe the Scots would be terribly nice to each other was taking naivety beyond the boundary of common sense.

But mine was not the prevailing view. Although Winnie Ewing in the chair on its first day declared that "the Scottish Parliament which adjourned on March 25th, 1707, is hereby reconvened," most saw it as brand new, and believed it would revitalise civic life, as well as dramatically changing and upgrading our economy and living standards. After all, the idea of bringing Scottish solutions to Scottish problems had been the foundation of the devolution movement. This new institution was to bring about a new society through new politics.

The new parliament could not have got off to a better start. The opening speech by Donald Dewar, the first First Minister, was brilliant, not only in its eloquence, but in spelling out the hope and belief that motivated generations:

This mace is a symbol of the great democratic traditions from which we draw our inspiration and our strength. At its head are inscribed the opening words of our founding statute: "There shall be a Scottish Parliament." Through long years, those words were first a hope, then a belief, then a promise. Now they are reality. This is a moment anchored in history. Today we reach back through the long haul to win this parliament, through the struggles of those who brought democracy to Scotland, to that other Parliament dissolved in controversy nearly three centuries ago. Today we look forward to the time when this moment will be seen as a turning point: the day when democracy was renewed in Scotland, when we revitalised our place in this our United Kingdom. This is more than about our politics and our law. This is about who we are, how we carry ourselves. In the quiet moments today, we might hear some echoes of the past: the shout of the welder in the din of the great Clyde shipyards, the speak of the Mearns, with its soul in the land, the discourse of the enlightenment when Edinburgh and Glasgow were a light held to the intellectual life of Europe, the wild cry of the Great Pipes, and back to the distant cries of the battles of Bruce and Wallace.

The past is part of us. But today there is a new voice in the in the land, the voice of a democratic Parliament. A voice to shape Scotland, a voice for the future. Walter Scott wrote that only a man with soul so dead could have no sense, no feel of his native land. For me, for any Scot, today is a proud moment: a new stage on a journey began long ago and which has no end. This is a proud day for all of us.

A Scottish Parliament. Not an end: a means to greater ends. And those too are part of our mace, woven into its symbolic thistles are these four words: Wisdom. Justice. Compassion. Integrity. At its head are inscribed the opening words of our founding statute: 'There shall be a Scottish Parliament.' Through long years, those words were first a hope, then a belief, Then a promise. Now they are reality.

This is a moment anchored in history. Today we reach back through the long haul to win this parliament, through the struggles of those who brought democracy to Scotland, to that other Parliament dissolved in controversy nearly three centuries ago. Today we look forward to the time when this moment will be seen as a turning point: the day when democracy was renewed in Scotland, when we revitalised our place in this our United Kingdom.

This is more than about our politics and our law. This is about who we are, how we carry ourselves. In the quiet moments today, we might hear some echoes of the past: the shout of the welder in the din of the great Clyde shipyards, the speak of the Mearns with its soul in the land, the discourse of the enlightenment when Edinburgh and Glasgow were a light held to the intellectual life of Europe, the wild cry of the Great Pipes, And back to the distant cries of the battles of Bruce and Wallace. The past is part of us, but today there is a new voice in the in the land, the voice of a democratic Parliament, a voice to shape Scotland, a voice for the future.

Walter Scott wrote that only a man with soul so dead could have no sense, no feel of his native land. For me, for any Scot, today is a proud moment: a new stage on a journey began long ago and which has no end. This is a proud day for all of us. A Scottish Parliament. Not an end but a means to greater ends. And those too are part of our mace. woven into its symbolic thistles are these four words: "Wisdom. Justice. Compassion. Integrity."

If anyone ever wonders why there is a statue of Donald Dewar in Glasgow, they should read that speech.

The question is whether the Parliament has met the high standard Donald set for it, and whether the belief so many invested in it has been met. How does it fare when we look at what twenty-six years have brought to our people? Has it transformed our economy and healed the scar of poverty that disfigures the face of Scotland? Has it sparked new life and vitality in our society?

And what about Wisdom, Justice, Compassion, and Integrity?

Too much was expected of too little

I don't think most people in Scotland, which includes those not born here but have been welcomed to settle in this nation, see the Scottish Parliament as having become a body sparkling with talent from which has poured forth imagination and transformative ideas. If it is measured against the expectations implicit in Donald Dewer's speech, it does not get a pass mark. That was bound to be the case.

Devolution corrected a fault in democracy that existed under the old system. Education, NHS, housing, social work, road infrastructure, and local government, had all been run for generations from St. Andrew's House in Edinburgh, by MPs elected to and responsible to the House of Commons. But the Government MPs who occupied those offices were often not from the party that most Scots voted for, and Scottish legislation was not always given the priority required in the Westminster Parliament's legislative timetable. Now, with devolution, the people could get the MSPs and the Government they voted for, and full legislative attention could be given to Scotland's domestic needs.

But the original 1998 Scotland Act did not endow the Scottish Parliament with economic powers that would give it the ability to act decisively on the reconstruction of the economy following the de-industrialisation in the years after 1980; until it was granted some powers to set and gain income tax revenue in the 2016 Act, its "budget" was in reality a distribution of a grant from Westminster. Even now, in 2025, some 50% of its income comes in the form of a Westminster allocation. In short, it may look like a government, and claim to be a government but it is not a government in the full sense of that word, because it is still minus the economic levers that can make a difference to economic performance. And if you do not have that ability, you cannot widen and deepen the economic base from which people become wealthier.

What went unnoticed during the passage of that Bill that became the 1998 Act, was that it was guillotined, with large parts of it never discussed. But that didn't matter to most, as long as the Parliament emerged and became a reality. I remember talking to people at the time, who were enraptured by the "new" and "different" congenial Parliament we were to have, but seemingly oblivious to the inadequacy of what was coming along with the title. What they expected could not happen.

I abstained in the 1997 referendum, after reading the White Paper that set out the powers the Parliament was to have, and not to have. I would not vote for what I knew was inadequate for the management of the Scottish economy. It was dubious if even the powers given in the 1998 Act were all they were cracked up to be. People with experience in the finance department of what was the Scottish Office told me that most of the budget, 90 per cent, was already pre-committed to services that were a statutory obligation – such as NHS, Education, local government (huge expenditure items), Police, Fire, roads, bridges, ports, and ferry services. The finance minister could tinker around with the figures, robbing Peter to pay Paul, but basically the budget was fixed. The discretionary amount available for new, innovative projects was around 10 per cent only.

Additions to the Parliament's power have been made since 1998, but none of the main levers of economic power have come north. On many an occasion, when John Swinney was finance minister, I would listen in astonishment as he boasted that Scotland, under his guidance, with the powers and the bloc grant at his disposable, would achieve greater GDP growth than the rest of the UK. Complete nonsense. He could have been blessed with the genius of Adam Smithand it would not have converted the impossible into the possible. The powers simply were not there and are not there now.

The MSPs have passed good Bills, as well as bad ones, and the Government has used its executive powers to implement policies at a pace not possible while Scotland was an integral part of the Westminster system.

But go back to the inspirational speech of Donald Dewar. The Parliament has been anything but an example of Wisdom, Justice, Compassion and Integrity. The events that led to the criminal prosecution of Alex Salmond, and how the parliament and its inquiry into how it lost the judicial review to him, has exposed a level of government incompetence, gross abuse of governmental power, corrosion of the professionalism and neutrality of the civil service -as well as revealing the lack of quality among the MSPs, many of whom seem to be unable to act with independent judgement.

It could be said that the Salmond affair is but one episode in twenty-six years. But what it revealed were huge flaws – cracks in the institution's structure and how its members are chosen by the parties and elected.

Our electoral system: the charter for Leaders' control.

The White Paper setting out the kind of Parliament it would be, opted for proportional representation. There are a number of PR systems. In Ireland a constituency will have three MPs, so the electors know who they are choosing. The Scottish one is a different route to PR: a combination of first past the post in a constituency (same as Westminster) with a top-up of seats for parties via the List, to produce the final total. Note the word "produce" rather than elect.

The constituency MSPs are definitely elected by the people. But it is really stretching "elected" too far to say those who become MSPs via the List, fall within a democratic definition. There are two types of list systems operating in democratic countries: the open one, with electors able to choose a person or persons from a list proposed by a party and a closed list, where the elector votes for the party, and gets who the party decides becomes an MSP. Scotland has the closed system.

In Scotland the party submits a list of people, numbered 1-12 to the returning officer in each region. Their names then appear in that order on the List ballot paper along with the party name and symbol, but it is essentially the party you vote for as the voter cannot change the order on which the names appear. It is highly doubtful if the voter knows all of them. In the May 2021 election in a number of regions prominent politicians were listed first and second, but if they won a constituency (being entitled to stand in both a constituency and the List) then the potential MSPs would be drawn from the rest of the List. After the constituency results are known, the returning officer declares who are the List winners.

Not all of the people on a party list have a chance of becoming an MSP. Occupying numbers 1 and 2 puts them in a good position, and in some regions a few that are lower down can find themselves blest. The SNP, in the 2015 election, won so many constituencies, that only four List MSPs were allocated to them. But that was not the case as the Parliament settled in during its early years.

Scotland's List system is a bad one. It breaches the principle that electors choose their parliamentary representatives on the basis of evaluating them as individuals as well as party candidates. It also gives party leaders the power of patronage and control. Not a fan of the leader? There is either no chance of being on the List, or a good chance of being too far down to get into Holyrood. Who is on the List, and their position on it, is how the party leaders either reward or punish people. Be a good loyalist, keep your mouth shut, vote as instructed, and you are on the best List position for the next election. Fail to follow that code of loyalty, think for yourself, speak out and even abstain or vote against, and you are out next time.

That is what happened to Margo MacDonald. No.1 on the List in Lothian in 1999, but deliberately placed way down in an impossible position for the election of 2003. So, she stood as an independent. Only she and Denis Canavan (ousted in 1999 from its candidates' list by Labour) could claim to be "elected" because only they, as independents, were named on the List as such. Denis won on the constituency vote and so did not need his List vote to make him an MSP.

The reasons why no others but those two made it as independents, are reputation, financial and organisational. Nothing stops anyone going on the List as an independent, and there are those who have done it, and there will be those who do it again. But the List is based on regions, not constituencies, and a region contains a number of constituencies. When Margo MacDonald stood in Lothian Region in 2003, there were nine constituencies with 360,000 voters. Huge amounts of money would normally be required for an independent candidate to run a campaign equal to that of the parties, something beyond any individual. Parties have substantial funds to fight elections, can muster armies of canvassers in each of those individual constituencies, and are armed with data gathered over the years about where their vote lies. An independent is just that, with little cash, no strong organisation to lean on, and no records to guide in campaigning.

Denis Canavan and Margo MacDonald could not compete in funding or organisation, but overcame those obstacles because they had long established national reputations for political quality, whom the people did not wish to see excluded from Parliament. They also commanded attention from the media, and so got free publicity that others could not command.

The closed List system has a malign effect on our Parliament. It is impossible in a Parliament drawn from a democracy for all representatives on the government back benches to be in such uniform agreement on everything, as happened for so many years on the SNP side of the Holyrood chamber, until recently. Some of them must have minds of their own. They must have been aware when mistakes were made. Yet, like the deputies in the Supreme Soviet of the USSR, all spoke and voted as one.

*

The existence and organisation of political parties is essential to the health of a modern democracy. A parliament of individuals would make the day-to-day task of dealing with the complex issues of today impossible. The role of a party is to bring within its tent many individuals who share broadly similar views and who can, working together, provide a government. For that government to work effectively, which requires it to have confidence in its continued existence, then it has to rely on its backbenchers being willing to compromise their own opinions and give support even when they are not in full agreement. The party system could not work otherwise.

There is an inherent problem with the party-in-parliament system, making it less than a perfect set up. If governments insist on backbench support on every occasion a vote is needed, then all individualism is squashed. If backbenchers

always comply with the instruction of the whips (and this applies to oppositions too) then it is sheep we have elected.

If backbenchers never rebel, or threaten to rebel, how are governments to be corrected before they make mistakes, or be made to reverse them? The relations in a parliament between those who form the government and those who sit and support it on the backbenches is crucial to how both perform in the public interest.

In practice, past and recent history of democratic legislatures shows that backbench individualism has not been crushed by the governments they maintain in office. At Westminster, in Canada, Australia, New Zealand, and the United States, governments have faced rebellions over Bills or their actions. There was until recently one exception: the Scottish Parliament's SNP backbench group.

That iron discipline imposed on SNP backbenchers was a direct result of the electoral system we have. That mindset of always complying with the leadership's instruction has remained in situ even when the SNP's seats came mostly from constituencies. The List has an additional flaw: a regional elected MSP regarded as useless by the voters in a region cannot be rejected at the next election, because if the party puts him/her at the top of the List, then re-election is guaranteed. That isn't the only flaw. If the person elected on the List dies or resigns, there is not a by-election and so no test during the parliament of the party's standing. The next one down becomes an MSP and the people get someone "representing" them in parliament that they have never known. Out of 129 MSPs, 56 are List ones – almost 43% of the total.

Change the electoral system and break the grip of the party leaders

What is the change required? Not first-past-the-post, if we want our Parliament to truly reflect how people voted. In the 2019 UK general election the SNP with 45% of the vote got 48 seats, leaving just 11 for all other parties. Labour with 18.6% had only 1 seat, whereas the LibDems with 9.5% had 4, and the Tories with 25% got 6.

We don't need to invent a new system of proportional representation to give us a Parliament more reflective of the voters' choice than the one operating for Westminster, or to overcome the obvious absurdities that the List system delivers. Since 2007, STV – single transferable vote – has been how we elect our local councillors in Scotland.

STV is used in Ireland, Northern Ireland, Malta, Australian Senate. It has the outstanding merit that should be the foundation of all electoral systems: it gives more power to the voter over parties and their candidates and it creates a direct link between those elected and the voters. That is the kind of democratic link that gives the person elected greater opportunity for individual expression of opinion and action, by invoking the views of his/her electors – the people who definitively put him/her in Parliament – in opposing his/her government when it is necessary to do so.

Chapter 15
For an independent Scottish Parliament we shall need quality – fewer of the "professional" class of politicians and more people with experience

In terms of formal education, with many having university degrees, today's MPs and MSPs are the best qualified bunch who have ever sat in any of the UK parliaments in modern times. But their dumb following of my leader, and their absence from the public sphere with few speeches and few articles, should make us wonder about the definition of "well educated" in the political context. A fair criticism is that they lack experience, that their belief in the mastery of spin is a weakness, and that their penchant for twittering with its severe limitation on communicating thought through only a limited number of characters is an insult to the public's intelligence.

The outstanding characteristic of the Holyrood Parliament is that a good number of its members lack both experience of life and expertise in the areas which make our society function. Where are the working-class shop stewards with years of dialogue and bargaining with employers? Where are the business people who know that to be an entrepreneur means taking an enormous risk? Where are the accountants who can fillet out the details of a PFI policy? Where are the engineers who can question why public sector contracts do or do not provide a road bridge that is operational in all days of winter? Where are the scientists who can question whether policies banning genetically modified crops are justified? Where are the people who can properly examine whether eliminating base load input of fossil fuels and nuclear, with greater long-term reliance on wind turbines, is a sensible energy generating policy? Where are the senior, and junior, university lecturers who can alert us to the damage being done to our intellectual life by our universities acting more like exploitative businesses than educational institutions?

There is a reason why they are not there, and it is not the fault of the political class, but the people. There is a latent public hostility to the numbers of people we put in Parliament, and that hostility grows exponentially when salary levels are considered. So, what I am going to write will be unpopular, but necessary.

There is no logic that can be applied to create perfect salary levels for elected politicians, and all attempts to settle on a system, independent pay review boards, or fixing them to salary levels in the civil service, stumble up against a public opinion that is hostile to what the media can depict as a "gravy train." A letter in the Edinburgh Evening News, 25th January 2021, headlined "Politicians can show worth with wage cut" is a fair example of the public's view of the politicians:

There are 650 MPs with a basic salary of £81,932. In addition there are about 800 politicians in the House of Lords and 129 Scottish MSPs. Add 1,227 local councillors in Scotland, about 20,000 in England and Wales and 462 in Northern Ireland and the cost of democracy becomes horrendous. Taxpayers are certainly not getting value for money. It is time for a cull of these numbers.

It would be easy and popular to agree about numbers and the other complaints made by this citizen from Linlithgow. However, leaving aside the House of Lords and considering that the UK has a population of 65m, with three distinct tiers of elected government, then the numbers are not horrendous nor are the salary levels outrageous. Indeed, as I argue in respect of the Holyrood Parliament, we need either more MSPs or a Senate for it to be effective. As for how our elected representatives can give better value for money, I come to that later.

*

The House of Commons scandal, when MPs milked their expenses, reinforced the hostility made plain in that Linlithgow letter. If the inner history of MPs' salaries and expenses was better known, people would see that fear of being seen to give themselves salary increases – even when recommended by an impartial outside review body – saw them opt for the less obvious expenses and thus ultimately open the way to fiddles.

There have been, even in the short life of the Scottish parliament, instances where the expenses system has been milked, not unlawfully, but unethically; this fuels the public antagonism to paid politicians.

If, however, we are to have a democracy that works in what is a technology driven revolution as profound in its consequences as was the industrial revolution (not to mention the rise of new global powers and a new world order), we need elected representatives capable of understanding and dealing with a complexity of issues far greater than faced by any generation before us. A full frank discussion is long overdue about how we pay our MPs and MSPs, and the experiences they should bring to governance. Nor can we ignore local government Councillors who are directly responsible for decisions that have a direct effect on the day-by-day lives of people.

There is much truth in the allegation that today's politicians being "professional" are the reason for a disconnect between them and the public, as evidenced by their obsession with gender and attacks on free speech, with even the then Scottish minister for justice backing a proposition that people can be prosecuted for hate crime speech for something said in the home. Just think of that for a moment. It is the kind of law Stalin used. That minister's CV showed him active in student politics, then as a researcher for an MSP, then becoming and MSP and on to ministerial cabinet level office. Experience? Judgement?

Professional politicians present in great numbers is only part of the problem in our democracy. As well as worrying about who is there in our parliament, we should also worry about who is not there. I was a participant in politics when manufacturing was king. In the House of Commons I first entered in 1970, there were on both sides of the chamber people who, before becoming MPs, had held a variety of jobs. Former Labour shop stewards would argue with former Tory managers, with both having experience of the industrial society that then existed. There were also foreign policy and defence experts. How many MPs at Westminster or MSPs in Edinburgh, have work experience in robotic engineering, artificial intelligence, life sciences, engineering, international trade, retailing, running a pub, restaurant or hotel, working in a supermarket, driving a train or bus, or laying bricks? How many working-class people have come straight from the private sector shop floor to the floor of Parliament?

Most of our politicians are "generalists," assumed to have the ability to absorb knowledge over a wide range of subjects, making them able to move from one ministerial post to a very different one as though they had some magic gift of understanding and mastering all things.

I am not arguing for a parliament with no generalists. If they are of calibre, and are equipped with the virtue of curiosity matched by intellectual rigour, and the ability to probe and question officials and their experts, then they are equipped for almost any ministry.

Take an English example: Michael Gove had a grip of the subject when education secretary of state in England, whereas his predecessor Gavin Williamson was out of his depth from day one.

Take a Scottish example, and ask why Alex Neil as Health Secretary has never come under fire for the NHS performance during his watch, when all others have been rated between poor and failure. The reason is that he had a background in international business long before he sought election and it showed immediately on his taking the job.

When he was appointed health minister, he swapped portfolios with Nicola Sturgeon. In the hand-over week, her private secretary stayed with him, and his with Nicola. At the end of the week, her private secretary told his that she was astonished by the number of questions he fired out at officials – demanding details on budgets, departmental policies, health board performances, and much else. He discovered, for example, that £50 million a year was being spent on HR consultants. Why do you need a consultant he asked, when you are in post because of your professional ability? No sensible reply. So that was cancelled. That was just one example of a minister with ability getting a grip. Ms. Sturgeon's private secretary, at the end of the turnover week, said her minister had never sent out anything like the stream of demands for information that flowed from his desk. Alex Neil is a socialist, but also someone with a business mind built on experience, whereas the quintessentially generalist Nicola Sturgeon, although a solicitor for a short time, was not. His generalist replacements have been nowhere near as competent.

The SNP did at one time have, as well as Alex Neil, an experienced businessman in its ministerial ranks – Jim Mathers who was an outstanding success. But he is long gone.

Chapter 16
Why we get what we've got

That brings me to why we have an overwhelming number of professional politicians and few in number who bring either experience or a particular expertise to the business of shaping public policy. There are scientific advisers within the civil service, as we have seen with Public Health Scotland, and there are civil service departments that have a responsibility for government policy towards business. But it would serve us better now, if among our elected representatives there were those able, from knowledge and experience, to challenge advisers.

There are good reasons, which should be a matter of grave concern, why scientists and others with technological and business knowledge (which includes workers who work in business) do not seek public office.

One is that a number cannot afford it. They can aim for much higher monetary awards as their careers advance, and with mortgages to pay and children to bring up, the cash is important. There are others. A political life is precarious; no sooner is someone elected than dozens of opponents work day and daily for him/her to lose the next election. Then there is the lack of privacy, with the lives of today's politicians turned inside out, and civility is replaced by viciousness on social media platforms. The last is no small matter. I know people who would now be able to stand for election, and who would make a valuable contribution to the Scottish Parliament, but will not submit themselves and their family to the lack of privacy and levels of abuse that have become normal.

On 4th February 2022, I was guest speaker at the Unison Lothian Health branch. It was a good mix of women, men, young people, and ethnic diversity. One hundred and fifty was the attendance. This was a group with a great deal of individual and collective experience of life. I asked how many had the ambition to become an MP or MSP. Only one. After the meeting, others came up and explained that their reluctance was due to the toxic nature of public life, and what they perceived as a belief among the people that politicians are not entitled to a private life. In my time as an MP in front line politics, I was confronted by a journalist who assumed the right to probe into my life. I gave him a blunt message for himself and his readers: “The public pay me, but they don’t own me.”

It will take a change in political culture to address that; we can do nothing about the precarious nature of the job, because electing and dismissing our MPs and MSPs is fundamental to a democracy. But we can change the other factors. If we want a wide range of experience and ability in our parliaments, then we need to admit we are not paying them enough and act on that admission.

I know it sticks in the craw for those on much lower wages than the MSP salary of £74,507 to argue for a higher one. But if we are the mature, intelligent society we believe ourselves to be, then we should be mature and intelligent enough to know that the present salary level is an impediment to having a legislature that can draw upon all the talents in our nation.

The answer to my argument is well known and it is the rule of the market: "If the salaries are not adequate, why do so many, hundreds, probably thousands, want to be MPs, MSPs and Councillors? The law of supply and demand applies to them as it does to turnips in the market. A big supply of turnips keeps the price down, just as the big supply of those seeking a parliamentary candidacy should keep the price of the prize title of MP, MSP, Councillor, down."

But there is however another rule of the market: you get what you pay for. For parliamentarians, it is the experience – the breadth and depth of knowledge – of those seeking the candidacies that matters. There is now a political class whose search for a special type of expertise is not the kind we need. They have mastered the parties' political systems on how to become a candidate and get into Parliament, for whom the present salary levels are ones not normally collected by people with such limited life experience.

Not all MSPs lack quality. There is a minority that are up to the job, but there are others there as are mere lobby fodder. This was made manifest, embarrassingly, in the way the Scottish Parliament and its "Committee on the Handling of Harassment Complaints" went about its business in what became known as "the Salmond Affair."

We had the embarrassment of watching the committee knuckle under to the Government it was investigating when the former refused to give them evidence asked for, refused to allow government witnesses to appear, and then allowed a government department – the Crown Office – to threaten prosecution of members of the committee if they published evidence that was already in the public domain. That was the same Crown Office with vital evidential material it refused to hand over.

Looking askance at this timid, gutless excuse for a Parliament, Lord Hope, a Scot, a former Deputy President of the Supreme Court and a man with many years on the Scottish bench, said witheringly that the Westminster Parliament would never have accepted such dictation. He did not need to add, that no government department, or prosecuting service, would have dared to threaten a House of Commons committee.

I suspect that all who watched the committee taking evidence from Alex Salmond were, like me, appalled by the calamitous lack of ability demonstrated by most of the committee members. The SNP ones, who must have been appointed as being among their best, were the worst. Only Jackie Baillie, the Labour MSP, and Andy Wightman, the Green MSP, gave us hope that not all our politicians were a national embarrassment.

Nothing summed up the ineptitude of parliament and its star committee, than when its witness, Alex Salmond himself, told them how they could get the evidence denied to them by the Crown Office. He pointed out that, as they knew, his lawyer had it, so all they had to do was issue his lawyer with a S23 order to hand it over. Weeks and months of wringing their weak hands, asking and getting rebuffed by the Crown Office, and having their requests flicked contemptuously aside – here at last someone told them how to go about their business. But, to no one's surprise, they did not exercise that power to compel the delivery of evidence. Yes indeed. We get what we pay for.

There is a way to improve on the level of mediocrity that avails us today. Both increase the salary level, and, as they do in the US Senate, allow MSPs to earn up to a limit from outside employment. That will enable people with experience who don't want to completely sever connection with their work, which they might need to return to fulltime if defeated in an election, to stand for Parliament.

I know the answer to outside employment will be that an MP and MSP job is a 24/7 one. Yes, an MP/MSP can be called upon at any time to address a constituent's or constituency problem, but that is not the same as the 24/7 claim implies. Look at the Westminster and Holyrood debating chambers: seldom full for debates on Bills. But what about committee work? That takes both study of papers and attendance to question witnesses, but the committees do not sit for a full day. Dr. Sandesh Gulhane MSP continues to practice as a GP, and there is no indication that in doing so he is any less effective than others. Indeed, he is the one worth listening to on health matters.

Then there is the question: what is the definition of a "second job," and how practical or impractical can it be for someone to fit a previous or new job in with legislative responsibilities? For a train, bus or HGV driver, or a shift worker in a supermarket, to take but a few examples, it might be difficult but not if the employer was willing to accommodate the job-parliament schedule. But it would not be difficult for a journalist, university lecturer, taxi driver, research scientist, someone running a family business, and quite a few others jobs where part-time work is the norm, to both work and be an MSP.

Adam Tomkins who served as an MSP from 2015-2020 was one of the most effective of that intake, while he continued to be a professor of law at Glasgow University. Back in the past, John P McIntosh was both an MP and Professor of politics at Edinburgh University.

Chapter 17
How does the Scottish Parliament work? Well, badly or needing improvement?

Too little attention has been paid to how the Parliament was organised from its first days, from which has flowed the present system of how many days it sits, how it organises them, the committee system, and the speaking time given to MSPs who take part in debates in the chamber. There is a kind of "taken for granted" view that it meets the needs of a modern democracy. I am far from sure about that.

The Parliament does not have the same range of powers as Westminster, but on subjects of importance in the domestic life of Scotland there are extensive powers, which the set-up and running of it do not accord with the needs of a vibrant democracy where, in the forum of the nation, we should see great issues addressed in depth.

For some in the SNP the word "Westminster" is toxic, and I anticipate any favourable comparison drawn between it and Holyrood to invite criticism. I wouldn't describe the House of Commons as the gold standard but it has been going a long time and has altered how it functions on several occasions to cope with changes as well as to ensure better scrutiny of government departments. To that end, it has strengthened its departmental oversight committees by having the chairs elected by a secret ballot of MPs – giving the chairpersons a more independent position and status, which in turn makes their committees more powerful. The UK government is required to respond to their reports (in 2025, a committee of the Scottish Parliament is now looking at the idea of committee chairs being elected, and paid, as in Westminster).

Westminster's rules on the time an MP can speak in a debate are not too restrictive, and ministers and opposition spokespersons are given ample time to develop their arguments.

There is a significant downside to how Westminster functions since I was last there. Many Bills are now timetabled: a softer guillotine lands on a Bill than the sharp one in my day, which was not a regular event. But the effect of the soft guillotine is the same, in that parts of Bills are never discussed either in committee or the chamber in the final stages. That makes for badly drafted legislation. But it does have a second chamber, the unelected House of Lords to revise Bills coming from the Commons. A job it does well.

How does that compare with Holyrood? Our Parliament is a 3-day week one: Tuesday, Wednesday and Thursday. Its hours are 9am to 5 pm, although it sometimes stretches to 7pm. Each of those working days, up to 1 pm, is taken up with committees either dealing with Bills or hearing witnesses on particular subjects. The time allocated to Ministers and MSPs in chamber debates does not encourage in-depth exploration of ideas and the philosophy or ideology that is inherent in a Bill or the subject that is under discussion. With the exception of the Programme for Government and the Budget, Ministers and their front bench opponents are given only eight minutes to speak, while backbenchers get four to six minutes, sometimes less than that. If there are any contemporary Scottish Michael Foots, Nye Bevans, Iain Macleods or Enoch Powells, all magnificent orators who dug deep into subjects, they would find the four to six minute rule equivalent to strangulation, and both the Parliament and public will be denied the kind of contributions that should be part and parcel of country's political life.

It is well known, and complained about privately within Holyrood, that too many MSPs come prepared with a speech written by a young researcher and just read it out. No original thinking. No real debate. Can anyone recall speeches made in a Holyrood chamber debate since 1999, that set the blood of the nation racing, inspired us, or that gave us a vision of what we could achieve?

Perhaps what I have written betrays my age, with a belief that a parliament is where a nation, through those it elects, meets to discuss, debate and thoroughly explore the issues that face the people and their society – where a clash of ideas is welcomed as intellectually invigorating. I wish Holyrood was that parliament, but it isn't.

The parliament we have now is not the creation of the Scottish people. It is a creature of statute – a statute made for it by the House of Commons. The original 1989 Act is worth reading. Leaving aside the issue of what powers were allocated, it is highly prescriptive – who can sit in it, how they are elected, how many MSPs, that it has a Corporate Body to run it, and even how it has to frame its standing orders. All that, of course was necessary in order that it was set up.

The 1997 referendum enabled the people to say they wanted a parliament, but Westminster decided what kind they would get.

We now need to address several questions. Are we as a nation content with what we have at Holyrood? If we are, but want it to work a bit better, how would we go about it? If we are not happy with it, and want big changes to how it is run and how it can be more significant for the nation, what are those changes? Are we able to agree on what changes we want, and if so, how do we get them? That last one falls into the devolution vs. independence context.

On the first question, I don't know about the nation, but I have no hesitation in saying the Scottish parliament is not working in the way that people hoped it would. That is my assessment from reading back to what people said in 1997, as compared to what has happened.

A three-day week, 9am-5pm parliament is an inadequate one. Its 129-person membership is not a large enough number to enable it to man an effective committee system. The committee system was supposed to avoid the need for a second chamber but its duality of a detailed legislative and investigation function, produces neither sound legislation nor consistently good reports that have a public impact. There is a rigidity in the way Parliament operates in its day-to-day life.

Outside of first minister's questions, its deliberations are not regularly reported on by the media.

If the independent Parliament is to assist Scotland's people to an understanding of the matters that determine how our economic life is shaped and how we face up to our responsibilities at the international level, it will have to be a very different one than that which operates at Holyrood under devolution.

Chapter 18
Upsides and downsides of a small country

The upside

The most successful countries at delivering a high standard of living are the small ones. From the World Population Review among the ten richest countries in the world nine are the small ones:

State	GDP Per Capita US$
Luxembourg	141,080
Switzerland	107,243
Ireland	107,243
Singapore	93,956
Norway	90,320
Iceland	90,111
USA	89,678
Qatar	72,760
Denmark	71,967
Australia	67, 979
With the UK much lower at	54,280.

Qatar cannot help being rich. It has the largest gas field in the world, with a population of 2.44m, and with only 12.10 per cent of that number actually being Qatari citizens; it is among this minority that the wealth is most lavished. The same could be said for Norway, with substantial oil and gas resources, and a population of 5.4m. It is Norway's size in relation to its oil resource that has allowed it to maximise it to good effect. Norway has a sovereign wealth fund of $1.738trn, the largest in the world in terms of total assets under management.

Switzerland, Iceland and Singapore do not have the kind of vast wealth resources enjoyed by Qatar and Norway, but they have been able to be innovative in building their economic base, and be nimble in policymaking in a world where recessional pressures have been experienced. Ireland's national income is precarious, with a heavy reliance on giant US corporations using it for tax saving purposes. It has placed its prosperity in the hands of others.

When the 2007-08 crash came, Alex Salmond's description of Ireland, Iceland and Norway as tiger economies looked false, as Ireland and Iceland in particular were severely damaged, and Norway's oil price fell. But all three bounced back more quickly than larger countries.

My nationalism, if such exists within me, is based on what Scotland could do economically if it became detached from its present position as an adjunct of the UK economy, where all the major economic powers and levers, and oil and gas resources, are not in our hands. That means we cannot strike our own priorities and cannot chart a different economic course from the slow lane we have been in for a very long time.

It is no accident that small countries are shown to be in the top league in tables of wealth and have outstanding reputations for the level of welfare enjoyed by their peoples. They can be so much quicker than large ones in adapting to changes in world economic conditions. Within each, the distance between the government and the people is much shorter, and so there is a greater chance of policies being more responsive to opportunity or need.

One of their assets is that most people in institutions, businesses, trade unions, the arts, or the law, either know each other or know of each other. This makes it easier to tap into the nation's talent when a national effort, or a national policy is needed.

That short distance between the centre of power and people is an advantage we have from Scotland's geography. For most of the population a short bus, train or car journey will take them to Edinburgh, and for others it is not a prohibitive distance to travel to see their MSPs, either to watch them in committee, the chamber, or come face-to-face with them on a particular issue. The old Scots saying applies: our fingernails can scratch them in Edinburgh but cannot reach to London.

Scotland's geography gives MSPs the chance to get around Scotland and see

and hear at firsthand how their policies are working or not: meeting communities, visiting schools, hospitals, care homes, small and large businesses, and building up knowledge for future legislation or executive action. That is how it should be and can be. There is some doubt if that is how it is with the present crop of MSPs in our devolved Parliament.

As other small states prove, when it comes to the test of wealth creation, swift adjustments to changing world conditions, gaining a high standard of living, and underpinning society with a protective welfare system, small works better than large.

But is there a downside?

To look at the possible downside of independence for the small nation of Scotland is not to damn that objective. It is to make sure that a downside will never be experienced again. There are lessons to be learned from the most recent years of our devolution politics, and it will strengthen the independence movement if it addresses them.

Supporters of independence are inspired by the belief that its achievement will transform Scotland on every count, economically and socially, into one of the most just and successful countries in Europe. That was the belief that sustained me and others in the fallow days of the SNP; it was the one conveyed at all the meetings I and others took part in on the Yes side in 2014.

I had no doubts. I have preached the importance of bringing intellectual rigour to bear on public policy, and on that important occasion, I failed to meet my own standard. I failed to examine the critical importance of the need for a constitution that secures balance through division of powers between government, parliament, the judicial system's absolute impartiality, and the people. I have been taught a lesson in the past few years.

I have not deserted my belief in what good independence can bring to Scotland's people, but it is necessary to confront doubts I had never previously contemplated, but have been compelled to do so by the way the SNP government has acted over the years.

My conception of an independent Scotland is one of open democracy, a pluralist polity, an effective parliament, an accountable executive government, and large measures of decentralised power to take account of the diverse nature of our land, islands, and population spread.

The events of what we call the "Salmond affair" from 2018 onwards made me realise that a small country can be "captured" by a governing party willing to misuse its powers and spread its tentacles of political corruption not only in parliament but into other institutions and civic society. Power is an elixir and is as capable in small as in large states of making its elites intoxicated and unbalanced.

Like others, I was shocked to discover that there appeared to be no brake on how the abuse of power was used against an individual citizen, and how that same power seemed to have subverted the ethical standards that make democracy different from the authoritarian/dictatorial regimes. They are:

Honesty by those with the power to be dishonest.
Restraint in the use of power by those in a position to abuse it.
Adhering to codes of justice by those with the power to ignore them.

Honesty, restraint, adhering to codes of justice, all were abandoned by the Scottish Government, MSPs who sought to defend the indefensible, the Crown Office, and sections of civil society for whom a jury's decision to clear Alex Salmond was unacceptable because they craved the opposite outcome.

A remarkable thing happened in the final stages of the parliamentary inquiry into the Salmond-Judicial Review case. While the members of the committee were questioning Nicola Sturgeon, who was giving evidence under oath and was therefore in a quasi-judicial forum, the Justice Secretary, Humza Yousaf, was tweeting derogatory comments about certain members of the committee who were questioning her. There was no thought of how he was damaging the integrity of the office he held and no sense of his office placing restraint on his conduct but what was worse was that it brought down no condemnation upon him or reprimand from within the governing party.

None of the editors of our national newspapers thought his conduct in that office worth editorial comment. Just as none of them thought to publish evidence to the inquiry by one of its main witnesses, in fear of the Crown Office. That it took a London-based political magazine, The *Spectator*, to publish the evidence and go to the Court of Session to have the law clarified, seemed to evince no signs of shame among our editorial corps. Once rot sets in, it spreads everywhere.

Those who wish Scotland to be a sovereign state, must ruthlessly examine and draw lessons from what has happened in our devolved statelet. That feature of a small country whereby so many at the top know each other, allows for the easy reach by government into civic society through central funding, thus making it open to "capture." This side of independence we have had a warning of what can happen.

So, in any future policy that is laid out for the people to consider as reason for making the decision to be in favour of independence, we must spell out the checks and balances that will prevent any one party in government capturing the new state.

We could start with whether we make good the claim that in Scotland the people are sovereign, with the text of a written constitution that declares and cements their rights as higher than the Government's and Parliament's.

One of the subjects that was rarely discussed in the 2014 campaign, and was not mentioned once in the

Scottish Government's 649 pages White Paper, *Scotland's Future*, nor in Stephen Maxwell's brilliant discourse *The Case for Left Wing Nationalism*, or my *In Place of Fear II*, was the importance of checks and balances, and the role in that of a written constitution. Drafting one should now be recognised as a priority. A number of people did work on this before 2014, but were largely ignored.

We should make one of the first clauses of a constitution the requirement for any person elected to the Parliament to swear an oath affirming that his/her first duty is to uphold the constitution, and place its requirements above that of the parliament, and any party, or faction within it. That oath should be a requirement for every Court of Session judge, Sheriff, Chief Constable, police constable, and the head and members of the Scottish armed forces.

Framing a written constitution is not a simple matter if it is to be the founding document of the new Scottish state. It will be important to divorce principles from policy. Some people I have talked to see it as a way of inserting policy that a government should have no way to avoid: the right to housing, the elimination of economic and social inequality, the elimination of poverty, the right to a living wage. These are all worth pursuing, but they constitute a list that if written on the tablet of a written constitution, would render government impossible.

In all states, governments face changing priorities over the years, and have to make decisions in favour of A as opposed to B, and C as opposed to both. So, if matters that are strictly policy are in a written constitution, they cannot all be met because they are policy and policy judgements are required on the allocation of resources, for which there is always competition.

It should – in a decent society – be possible to house people, abolish poverty, manage the economy and labour market so that good wage levels are the norm, but the ability to do so depends on economic factors and the wealth-creating performance of such a society, and that cannot be commanded by words in a constitution – only from the application of energy and ideas of the people, and policy choices by government about macro-economic management and distribution of the economic dividend.

Chapter 19
Our Cities, Towns and Countryside
The often ignored part of our government

Local government does not arouse the same interest as national elections, or in what local councils do, compared to events in Parliament. A good year for voter turnout is 47%, but even that figure hides some depressing lows. Glasgow barely makes 40%. Some 2.3m Scots don't vote in local elections.

Yet, in many respects local government could be said to be more important in the lives of people than parliament. While Holyrood legislates, the government has no direct day-to-day executive control over how a number of its Acts are applied. It uses other organisations. The NHS and Education are good examples: the former is delivered by health boards and other organisations, and the latter by local authorities. Social work and care of the elderly is another where Parliament legislates, the Scottish Government allocates resources, but local councils do the implementation.

One of the merits of Ben Thomson's *Home Rule*, was his identification of how devolution has brought greater power for central government in Scotland while diminishing it at the level of local authorities. There has been no bonfire of the Quangos; we have seen instead a steady burning off of the areas in which local government is able to exercise autonomy and there has been a stark failure to recognise that the significant differences between the Highlands, the Islands, the borders, Grampian, Dumfries, Galloway and the central belt call for more local powers of decision and less central government dictation.

When I was in the House of Commons, on the Labour benches, and devolution became a possibility, I recall saying that it meant the day of the centralisers was over. That turned out not to be true in devolved Scotland. Looking at how the Scottish Government has employed its powers, the impression is that it knows better than councillors, and in Quangoland it appoints people who are convinced they definitely know better than councillors and others.

Take the example of ferry services to the Western islands, the lifeline for all who live and work there. Should those communities through their local councils not be the ones to decide what kind of vessels they need, and all else that goes to make up those services? Why does the Scottish government think that by appointing a Danish businessman as head of CalMac, rather than people from the Western Isles, it is more likely to produce an effective ferry service? Why is there no-one from the islands on the board of CalMac? There is no answer to the question of whether the ferry fiasco – the inability to deliver two of them on time – would have occurred if the set-up between Cemal and Ferguson's yard had been controlled by the local councils. But it is question worth asking.

Who knows better than those who live and work locally what they need? Why, for example, should the communities in the inner and out Hebrides, and

Arran, not own and manage CalMac rather than the Scottish Government and its quangos? Or take another example: why is Prestwick airport owned by a Scottish Government which seems clueless about what to do with it, at a cost of £50m so far, rather than being in the hands of the local council who could see it as an asset to be exploited not just as an airport?

Glasgow is not Shetland, Edinburgh is not Peebles, Galloway is not Lanarkshire, Stornoway is not Dundee, Inverness is not Aberdeen, Arran is not Forfar, and power should be devolved from Holyrood to enable them, and all others, to decide and act on their local priorities.

There is a rich Quangoland to be redistributed to local government. Perhaps it is time for local council leaders to change course, and instead of complaining about the powers that have been drained from them, start to assert that they should be restored and new powers given that would enable them to better serve their communities. Scotland is central-belt centric at present. That has to change.

One of the changes that should be made is the dismantling of Police Scotland with the restoration of local government control, on a Joint Board basis, producing six or seven Police Forces. There are democratic grounds for not having the coercive arm of civil government, the Police, as a single force. It gives too much power to a single individual and institution. Policing by consent is best at a local level, with oversight from councillors who have a democratic mandate for that purpose.

Before leaving local government, I will venture into two relevant areas not touched upon by Ben Thomson's *Home Rule*. First is to ask and answer the question "How extensive is the time demand on councillors, and are they paid enough at a level that would attract as wide a possible range of people to serve on councils?"

In the 1950 and 1960s Councillors were all part-time, with working class members remunerated only for any money lost through deduction of wages by employers when attending daytime meetings. Business people got no payments, other than reimbursement of travel costs. Some councils and committees met at night. The range of responsibilities were much fewer than those exercised by councils today.

I can find no surveys of how many part-time councillors serve today, and I expect a fair number are full-time. The pay, subsistence and transport reimbursement levels are set by the Scottish government. There are four salary grades: Council Leader, Civic Head, Senior Councillor, and Councillor. Councils themselves are graded according to size with, for example, Leader salaries ranging from £35,580 for East Lothian to £64,043 for Glasgow and Edinburgh. The ordinary Councillor receives a salary of £21,345. I cannot find any council that meets at night, so that last figure is likely to be for a full-time Councillor.

The Leaders of all local council have jobs which are as demanding on a 24/7 basis as any MP or MSP. Some will have heavier burdens than others. A city like Glasgow, a highly concentrated urban environment, will generate problems to be tackled on a scale not matched by an islands council, hence the grading of salaries.

An MP and MSP both have legislative responsibilities, but unless they are in government, they do not have executive power. Councillors make decisions that have direct effect on the people in their areas.

To recognise the importance of local government, and the efforts made by Councillors, pay at 75% of an MSP's salary level for all, with an additional sum for Leaders, and Civic Heads, alongside a top-up for Glasgow and Edinburgh would seem to be appropriate and proportional to their responsibilities.

The national media spotlight seldom shines upon a local councillor, although reporting on council business in the local press provides valuable information to the local people. But where are the national figures that used to stride across that turf or council leaders and opposition figures who could command public attention and could make government ministers sit up and take note? They were the giants of local government.

They used to exist. Ayrshire had Danny Sim. Renfrewshire Dr. McFarlane. Glasgow produced Pat Dollan, Donald Liddle, Bill Gray, Michel Kelly, Pat Lally. Strathclyde produced Geoff Shaw, Dick Stewart and Charlie Gray. Edinburgh was notable for Cornelius Waugh, Jack Kane, Eric Milligan and Peter Wilson when he led Lothian region. These were giants in the past. Where are those of the present? As the powers of local government have disappeared so has the national platform for its present leaders.

Local government also carries a political unfairness. Its members pay the political price for the failures of the national parties they are members of. I have seen good councillors of all parties dismissed by an electorate who were judging their national leaders rather than the councillors had been doing.

I confess, I don't know the immediate answer to this. Local elections are taken as a barometer of how national parties are doing all over Europe, and elsewhere. It happens elsewhere. In the USA, a contest for a Wisconsin Supreme Court judicial position was held to be an early test of approval or disapproval of the

Trump-Musk administration. In Scotland, if Councils regain old powers and new ones, and their leaders become once again national figures that are able to convey the value of local government, there could be a better and fairer judgment of them. Perhaps.

Chapter 20
The post-independence question
Where does Scotland fit itself in Europe?

Our long membership of the European Union, and the vote on Brexit, has left a difficult legacy that will have to be addressed. The SNP has glued a vote for independence to joining the EU. That policy is always stated as re-entry but in hard legal fact it means Scotland, as a state, would be a new applicant. It was reported in January 2022 that a number within the SNP want to make the question of EU membership separate from a vote on independence. I hope they succeed.

I don't say that because I voted Leave. First of all, there is no guarantee that re-entry would be as easy as some think. The EU has poured kind words on the Scottish Government when using it as a foil in its spats with the Boris Johnson administration. However, there has not been even a nuanced official hint that, post-independence, an application to join would be given a smooth path with no prices attached. The EU is not a benevolent society, and would judge any Scottish application in relation to its own interests, as well as those of its member states. If a price for re-entry was joining the euro, then the sovereignty just won would be transferred out. That is a possibility. Then there is a veto by Spain, always there in the background, for whom

"Scotland" means "Catalonia". It is difficult to see how Scottish waters could avoid re-entry to the Common Fisheries Policy; the temptation for the EU to extend its competence to the Scottish oil and gas fields would be great, given it tried that ploy with Norway in 2012, only to have its effort rebutted by that EFTA sovereign state.

What to do about Europe is not just an issue for the SNP but for all parties. Just over a million voted Leave and when the real time consequences of going back into the Lisbon treaty are recognised, they and others are unlikely to shift their opinions.

The question we have to answer is: what do we want for Scotland in our relations with the EU? Easy access to its markets is obvious but there are many who want a closer relationship than just another one of the countries it trades with. The one policy that probably will meet the different points of view is for an independent Scotland to join EFTA and through it the European Economic Area, which brings not just easier trade but cooperation, free movement of people and capital, and a constant working dialogue on new laws affecting the single market.

That would take Scotland, like Norway, into the EU single market but also keep it out of other areas where we would regard the exercise of sovereignty, free from other influences, as vital.

There is an oft repeated canard that Norway and EFTA states just do what the EU instructs, but that is not so. EFTA countries remain sovereign states. As I pointed out in a pamphlet in 2016, between 2000 and 2013, Norway adopted 4,724 EU laws, whereas in those years member states of the EU adopted 52,183 EU laws.

Anyone can see why there is that difference by reading the text of the EEA agreement, particularly Articles 99 and 100. They, and other Articles creating the EEA institutions, prevent Norway becoming a submissive state and reinforce its status as a sovereign nation.

But however tempting that EFTA policy is, it has to be re-assessed in the Brexit context that places England outside the EU customs union. That England and the other parts of the UK will continue to be our largest export market cannot be ignored. Would EFTA entry require a trade border with England? Would the twenty-seven EU states in the EEA allow Scotland to have a different agreement with England on the border than it has allowed in the Brexit withdrawal agreement in respect of Northern Ireland?

There is another factor that has to be recognised: entry to EFTA is one thing, but entry to the European Economic Area is quite another. EFTA could propose Scotland for membership of the EEA, but acceptance by the EU side would require unanimous agreement of all twenty-seven EU governments and individual parliaments. Would Spain see us in that context as being sui generis, and not a Catalonia stocking horse?

There is a great deal of work to be undertaken in examining the external relations options for an independent Scotland before we ask the people to vote on the issue of where we might, or might not, align ourselves in terms of trade agreements and political partnership.

Conclusion

If the independence movement is to win, then we need to face facts that cannot be avoided, not least those that raise the question of the SNP's future role. The better the lessons learned and the better our position is thought out, the greater strength the cause will have in persuading the people to vote for it.

Some of what I have written will upset people, a good number of them people with whom I share a commitment to gaining Scottish independence. I may, and hope I have, upset Devo-Max enthusiasts by pointing out that however it is dressed up, it is still devolution with limits placed on the Scottish Parliament.

My intention has not been to upset as many as possible, or to be rude, but to try and persuade people of goodwill, from every position, that there is a clamant need to examine the governance of Scotland now, how we came to it, the quality of our elected representatives, what has gone wrong with the Parliament and why; moreover, that they should accept that there is a common interest for all in ensuring that if independence does come, the model we build the new Scotland upon has solid, enduring democratic foundations.

Epilogue
The Labour Party in Scotland
Why it needs to become, dare I say it, a real Scottish Labour Party

The Labour party and its voters are important in decisions about Scotland's constitutional position, and it, along with other socialist parties, has an ideological problem with the National Question.

Scottish Labour has been unable to resolve that Question and that failure was both at the root of its defeat post-2014 and the reason its struggles to recover have not succeeded. The National Question is essentially this: *socialism is an economic answer to international capitalism, and therefore requires for its success action by workers in concert with other workers across state boundaries, but how does that square with the primary loyalty working class people show to their nation states? A loyalty that can make a nation's state issues their priority along with others within that state whose class interests are not theirs?*

Does not a working-class Scot have more in common with a worker in Liverpool, and elsewhere, than with the Duke of Buccleuch or a Scot in charge of a bank? Capitalism is international, socialist action has to be the same, and so, ipso facto, nationalism is the antitheses of socialist belief and has to be rejected.

That theoretical proposition of who a Scottish worker has most in common with is true in terms of the universal relationship of capital and labour but the message of the theory is not reflected in the reality of how human beings think and the social and historical magnetic points to which they refer in shaping their conception of themselves within and as a nation. The theory takes no account of history and its formulation of nations and cannot recognise that, however unlikely it would seem on the surface, the working-class Scot does have things in common with the duke and others of different classes. Strands of history and culture, and the importance of certain common events, even ones of antagonism between classes at different times, create commonalities of thought and interest across the classes in Scotland.

Our pre- and post-reformation religious history is replete with cross-class interaction, common purpose, and sacrifice. The works of Robert Burns are embraced by every class in Scotland. Although not everyone in every class has sought adjustments to the 1707 agreement, people from every class have done so and have continued to do so. Home Rule was not a side issue only for the ILP, or the Liberals when they were dominant in Scotland. The working class, like the other classes, are part of what all see as the Scottish nation.

The reality between the socialist internationalist theory and the reality of what people think and do presents a conundrum to Scottish Labour members. I have been in the same place. Those of us who set up the SLP in 1976 wrestled with it, and I and others had what I have described as a slow-burn conversion from unionist to devolutionist to advocate for independence. It was not an easy journey, but we found it a necessary one if we were to prioritise the need for the Scottish working class to sell their labour dearly and enjoy a level of prosperity for all that had so far eluded us under the union. I personally found some comfort along the way from the words of Nye Bevan that "If you want to change the world, it is not a bad idea to start on your own doorstep."

What at root ails the Labour party up here, is its lack of Scottish authenticity. It lives under the rules of the British Labour party. It is a subservient, not autonomous, part of that party. It takes that party's whip in the House of Commons. Its spokespeople there are appointed by the leader of that party, and while it has room in the Holyrood parliament to respond to Scottish policy issues and events, it cannot take a position on major matters or the UK constitution that differs from that party. It seeks to pretend that it is more than just a "branch" of UK Labour but does not succeed. It does not fully fund itself, is not fully in charge of policy which, at Westminster elections, sees it Scottify but make no real change to the manifesto written by its boss – the UK National Executive.

In the final analysis, that it has to conform to what the UK leadership tells it to believe, is Scottish Labour's crippling weakness. Neil Findlay and David Martin have talked, without detail, about more powers for Holyrood, as has Sir Keir Starmer, but everyone knows it is the latter as Leader and the NEC that supports him, who are in control and who will set such powers out and require its Scottish component to comply.

That is the hard fact of the relationship. Are Labour party members in Scotland willing to put up with this non-autonomous, policy-restricting position, even if it means more defeats?

Is Scottish Labour looking honestly at the basic cause of its decline – its failure on the constitutional question – as it is unable to strike in a new direction of independence within the British Labour movement? The ideological ties that bind the party's leadership to the UK unionist party may remain unbroken. If that is so, then the next time Scots have to decide their future the leaders will again find themselves at odds with their voters.

Appendix

Powers for the UK and Scotland set out by Ben Thomson's *Home Rule*
("Reservations" are the powers given to each Parliament)
"Summary of UK Parliament powers Under a Home Rule Settlement"

General Reservations:

- Constitution (Crown, union, UK Parliament)
- Registration and funding of UK political parties
- International relations
- International development
- Regulation of international trade
- UK civil service
- Defence
- Treason

Specific Reservations:

- Head A. Financial and Economic Matters
- Fiscal policy (power to raise and collect taxes in Scotland to meet UK expenditure in, and on behalf of, Scotland and administer a redistribution fund)
- Economic policy (ensuring UK single market operates efficiently, with free movement of goods, services, capital and people based on principle of mutual recognition)
- Monetary policy (macro-economic management, including growth and stability fund)

- Currency

Head B. Home Affairs

- UK elections
- Immigration and nationality
- National security, official secrets and terrorism
- Emergency powers
- Extradition
- Access to non-Scottish public bodies.

Head L. Miscellaneous

- Control of nuclear, biological and chemical weapons and other weapons of mass destruction
- Time
- Outer space
- Antarctica

"Summary of New Scottish Parliament Powers Under Home Rule Settlement"

General Reservations:

- Responsibility for the existence of the High Court of Justiciary and Court of Session
- Registration and funding of Scottish political parties
- Scottish civil service

Specific Reservations

Head A. Financial and Economic Matters (power to raise taxes and borrow, *within limits*, to meet Scottish expenditure – financial services, financial markets, money laundering). (emphasis added)

Head B. Home Affairs (misuse of drugs, data protection and access to information, firearms, entertainment, scientific procedures on live animals, betting and gaming and lotteries, lieutenancies).

Head C. Trade and Industry (business associations, insolvency, competition, intellectual property, *import and export control,* sea fishing outside the Scottish zone, consumer protection, product standards, safety and liability, weight and measures, telecommunications, postal services, research councils, designation of assisted areas, industrial development, protection of trade and economic interests).

Head D. Energy (electricity, oil, gas, coal, nuclear energy, energy conservation).

Head E. Transport (road, marine and air transport)

Head F. Social Security (non-devolved social security schemes, child support. pensions).

Head G. Regulation of the Professions (architects, health professions and auditors).

Head H. Employment (employment and industrial relations, health and safety, non-devolved job search and support).

Head J. Health and Medicines (xenotransplantation, embryology, surrogacy and genetics, medicines, medical supplies and poisons, welfare foods).

Head K. Media and Culture (broadcasting, public lending right, government indemnity scheme and property accepted in satisfaction of tax).

Head L. Miscellaneous (judicial remuneration, equal opportunities, Ordnance Survey).